1 How happy are those
who live according tc

2 Happy are those who keep His decrees
and seek Him with all their heart.
3 They do nothing wrong;
they follow His ways.
4 You have commanded that Your precepts
be diligently kept.
5 If only my ways were committed
to keeping Your statutes!
6 Then I would not be ashamed
when I think about all Your commands.
7 I will praise You with a sincere heart
when I learn Your righteous judgments.
8 I will keep Your statutes;
never abandon me.

9 How can a young man keep his way pure?
By keeping Your word.
10 I have sought You with all my heart;
don't let me wander from Your commands.
11 I have treasured Your word in my heart
so that I may not sin against You.
12 LORD, may You be praised;
teach me Your statutes.
13 With my lips I proclaim
all the judgments from Your mouth.
14 I rejoice in the way revealed by Your decrees
as much as in all riches.
15 I will meditate on Your precepts
and think about Your ways.
16 I will delight in Your statutes;
I will not forget Your word.

Psalm 119:1-16 (HCSB)

Discover the Bible

A Guide to Finding Meaning and Significance in God's Word

Josh Shoemaker

Biblical Framework Press

Discover the Bible: A Guide to Finding Meaning and Significance in God's Word

Published in Phoenix, AZ by Biblical Framework Press.

Cover Design: Travis Vasquez

Illustrations: Katie Saltzman

Paperback ISBN: 978-0-9858958-2-2
Electronic ISBN: 978-0-9858958-3-9

This book is dedicated to Rich Thune, a friend and mentor. Thank you Rich, for teaching me, through your wisdom and example, to have a deep reverence for God's Word.

Contents

Translations and Versions of the Bible referred to in this book

AMP	The Amplified Bible
ASV	American Standard Version
CEB	Common English Bible
ESV	English Standard Version
GNT	Good News Translation
GW	God's Word Translation
HCSB	Holman Christian Standard Bible
KJV	King James Version
MSG	The Message
NAB	New American Bible
NASB	New American Standard Bible
NCV	New Century Version
NET	New English Translation
NIrV	New International Readers Version
NIV	New International Version, 2011
NIV '84	New International Version, 1984
NJB	New Jerusalem Bible
NKJV	New King James Version
NLT	New Living Translation
RSV	Revised Standard Version
TLB	The Living Bible
YLT	Young's Literal Translation

Preface

I love God.

Love Him!

And for whatever reason, He has placed proper Bible interpretation as a passion in my heart. I've been blessed to teach it many times to a number of people over the years, in both small groups and in the academic setting of a university. I truly feel that there is no more important subject that I could teach to other believers in Christ.

While many people have influenced my thinking, an especially big thank you goes to the following people whose courses, podcasts, papers, discussions or books have greatly influenced my understanding of Bible interpretation: Greg Koukl, Ben Shin, Walt Russell, Scott Duvall, Daniel Hayes, Scott Smith, Gordon Fee and Douglas Stewart.

The idea of this book originated while doing an assignment for my hermeneutics (that just a fancy word for Bible interpretation) class at Biola, where we were required to develop a training program to pass on what we'd learned. So, this book originally began as a PowerPoint presentation with notes and over the years has developed into its current state.

Through that time, I've had the opportunity to read many books on Bible interpretation. There are typically two types of hermeneutics books that I encounter.

First, there are the text books (and similar books that might as well be textbooks) which are used in the classrooms of Bible colleges. These books contain detailed material on how to properly interpret the Word of God. And while there are a number of fantastic resources available, many people find that to read these books effectively often requires either prerequisites or considerable supplemental study.

Second, there are the more popular books on understanding the Bible. Once again, there are many good options available. However, these mainstream books on interpretation frequently lack the depth that many Christians today are looking for. They're great for a basic introduction, but readers may feel left wanting something more, something that tells them why, not just how.

I've put this book together for the territory in between. It's for those that want the academic tools and understanding, but written in such a way to make it accessible to almost anyone. I pray that your Bible study, and thus your relationship with our God, is enhanced through the lessons in this book.

It is all for His glory.

Acknowledgements

So many people have helped me along this journey, either by being the subjects as I taught through the material, or directly helping me with the finished copy. Their input has been incredibly valuable, and this book would be nowhere near what it is today without their help and encouragement.

I want to thank everyone from my small groups at Cornerstone in Chandler, AZ where I first taught this material. The discussions from those nights helped shape this from a school project into a rough outline for the book. I miss you all and you are often in my thoughts. PS–Sorry April, but there's nothing in here on Hebrews 6:4-6. :-)

I also want to thank the guys in mo(men)tum who met with me for a couple weeks over at Bill's house to go over some of the first finished chapters: Bill Arsenault, Alex Cabrera, Bryan Matsuyoshi, Daren DeShon and Jon Moyer. Thanks for offering your thoughts to the early parts of the book.

Thanks to Sandi Gray who offered feedback on a couple of chapters. You and Scott are amazing friends and I cherished your encouragement to me to write this book over the many years it took me to complete it.

Thanks to Adam Reed, for challenging me to get off my fanny and finish this thing.

Thank you to Katie Saltzman for your artistic skills and providing the illustrations.

I am grateful to John Correia for offering feedback on parts of the book and also for helping me with the process of getting it to print.

Special thanks goes Gary Braness, Tom Skawski II and Joe Gorra who each read and edited the entire manuscript. Gentlemen, I am so grateful for your feedback.

Thanks to my parents who encouraged me and for all the babysitting you did for us during the process.

Thank you to my awesome family for enduring all those times when I went to be in my office. To my amazing wife, Shannon, I could never have finished this without you. I am so blessed to have you as a partner.

And thank you to God in Heaven who saved me, allowed me to be a member of your Kingdom, and blessed me with the honor of writing this book.

Introduction

When I was a boy, my family would get together for Easter to celebrate in a large group at my aunt's farm. The best part of those gatherings was the egg hunt. My cousins and I would wait in anticipation as the grown-ups hid all the eggs, often in some really tricky places. Then at the moment my aunt shouted "Go!" we'd scatter like fireworks, bursting out in all directions. It was such a thrill to find those little plastic eggs filled with special candy treats! Sometimes they would rattle with the clanging sound of a few coins, and perhaps even a fifty cent piece. We were in pure bliss as we sprinted around the yard hunting for those hidden treasures!

For Christians, in many ways reading the Bible is like searching for treasure. The pages of Scripture are filled with our Savior's truths that just need to be discovered. Packed with stories and songs of love, hope, adventure and purpose, it is God's revelation to mankind. It is His story for the world, the world He loved so much that He sent His beloved Son to die for. He gave us this book to teach us about who He is and our relationship to Him. It's a guidebook to life. It's a love letter from our Creator. It's a tangible connection to the hope we have. It's all of that, and much, much more. It is indeed a treasure.

The Purpose of This Book

Most of the time, in order to find a treasure, we need a good and reliable map. The map tells us the location of the treasure. X marks the spot. But having the map alone won't get us there. We also need to be able to read and understand the map, or we could wind up lost.

One of the most rewarding endeavors we can do as followers of Christ is to equip ourselves with the right tools to help us properly interpret and apply the teachings within the pages of Scripture, so that on our own, we can discover the treasure.[1] We need to learn to read the Bible correctly. Just like reading a map wrong can take us way off course, the same can be true if we don't read the Bible accurately. And it's often not a simple task.

Much of the Bible is foreign to us. It's a different time, a different place, a different people and a different language. One of the aims of this book is to teach us how to cross that bridge of time, place, people and language so that we can gain a better understanding of the Bible and help bring it more to life for us. The ultimate goal we're after is our own personal transformation.[2] We want to know God more and be transformed by Him. His Word is an instrument for that change.

---

[1] Before you jump ahead, I'm not suggesting that we interpret the Bible as if alone on our own island, discovering what it means to us individually. On the contrary, this book is about how to discover the true meaning of the Word that is accessible to everyone. We will discuss how we can use the vast material available to us from authors of the past and present. We will learn how to use the tools available without relying on someone else to *tell us* what the Bible means, but we will certainly not neglect the insights of scholars and historians before us.

[2] And by this God is glorified.

Our Father has given us this wonderful collection, full of His wisdom. He wants us to explore it, and to learn from it. He knows that when we follow the wisdom in its pages, we will be protected from the world and we will grow closer to Him. Note the father's instruction to his son in Proverbs chapter 2:

> My child, listen to what I say and remember what I command you. Listen carefully to wisdom; set your mind on understanding. Cry out for wisdom, and beg for understanding. Search for it like silver, and hunt for it like hidden treasure. Then you will understand respect for the Lord, and you will find that you know God. (NCV)

To discover the wisdom in the pages of Scripture, we need to have the proper tools.[3] The tools we will learn in this book will help us discern what the Bible teaches and help us to be confident we are on the path to truth. Then, equipped with the right know-how, we can be like an explorer starting a glorious and daring journey to find the greatest treasure of all time.

---

[3] I am not suggesting that the Bible is only understood by the academic elite who have learned the tools of proper interpretation. In fact, I totally agree with this statement from the 1689 Baptist Confession of Faith (Chapter 1, Paragraph 7) "All things in Scripture are not alike plain in themselves, nor alike clear unto all; yet those things which are necessary to be known, believed and observed for salvation, are so clearly propounded and opened in some place of Scripture or other, that not only the learned, but the unlearned, in a due use of ordinary means, may attain to a sufficient understanding of them." (see www.1689.com/confession.html#Ch.%201) All people can understand the essentials of Scripture. This book is about diving deeper. It is about learning to discern those things which are not as plain and not as clear, so that we can continue to grow in our walk with God.

No Pain, No Gain

Sometimes discovering something new can be hard on us. I was seven when I learned the truth about Santa Claus. (Warning: Santa spoilers ahead.) Like most people, I found out from the older kids at school. After spending the day standing up for the old man in the red suit 'til I was blue in the face, I finally began to have doubts. That afternoon I went home and trepidatiously asked my mom, "Is Santa…real?" To my grave disappointment, I got the truth. Oh, and it hurt. I remember crying my eyes out at the kitchen table when she confirmed that Santa was indeed a fiction.

I really loved Jolly Old Saint Nick. He wasn't just a guy who showed up with presents when I was good – he was part of my world, what was real to me. And now I knew it was all fake: the North Pole, the flying reindeer, the elves and the joy and happiness brought with every "Ho! Ho! Ho!" Of course time went by, and just like every other kid, I recovered. I even went on the following year to be one of those rotten kids who made fun of the ones who still believed, and I no doubt sent many of them home crying to their mothers.

I bring this story up to caution us as we embark on this study of Biblical interpretation. As followers of Christ, the Bible is special to us and any time our beliefs about it are either confirmed or challenged, we're going to be passionate about it. As you read through this book, some of you will agree (and want to give copies to all your friends), and others will be angry (which is why my address isn't included), but I suspect many of you will feel like you did when you learned that Santa wasn't real. You won't want to believe it, you'll fight it, you'll be confused about what you thought was real, and it might even hurt a little. But remember, learning that Santa was not real also opened your eyes to the truth. So please hang in there with me to see what may be uncovered. In the end, you may just walk away feeling like you learned something valuable and useful.

Dissecting Sacred Cows

When we hear the term "sacred cow," many of us might think of Moses coming down the mountain and seeing the sinful act of the nation of Israel worshipping a golden calf. But that's not what is meant by the term. A "sacred cow" is actually a figure of speech describing a particular view that is "unreasonably held to be beyond criticism."[4] In other words, something becomes a "sacred cow" if the bearer of the view won't listen to any reasonable counter ideas or views.

In order to make our study together in this book more interesting and hopefully more memorable, we'll be looking at some Scripture passages that are often misunderstood – a few even so overly misused that we've adopted the mistreatment into our art, music and sometimes even our sermons. For some of us, it might even be a favorite verse, a "sacred cow," which is going to make us a little uncomfortable. Hopefully, if I've done a good job of accurately handling the Word, you'll feel like you learned the correct meaning. Still, ultimately my goal is not to convince you that my interpretations of certain Scripture passages are correct, but rather to illustrate for you good principles for interpreting Scripture on your own.

My son has a good way of describing times like this when you learn something that is counter to what you've always thought. He says it's like trying to swallow bubble gum flavored

---

[4] "sacred cow." *Collins English Dictionary - Complete & Unabridged 10th Edition.* HarperCollins Publishers. 04 Jan. 2011.

candy. Even if your brain knows it's right (because its candy), until you get used to the new idea (that you can swallow something both solid and gum flavored), your instincts based on past experience make you want to stop it from going down. So as you read, if you feel uncomfortable, my request is that you ask yourself this question: "Am I feeling discomfort because this is counter to Scripture or am I feeling this way because something I was used to and valued is being taken away from me and I'm having a hard time with it." Let's remember to "test all things and hold fast to what is good" (1 Thess. 5:21).

What to Expect

One other item should be noted before we begin. I've tried to write this much differently than a standard Bible interpretation book. The "sacred cows" are one element of that. I've also tried to include in most chapters, not only an interpretive principle, but a practical application related to the passage or passages that the principle deals with. This approach takes away some of the typical "textiness" normally found in a book on Bible interpretation.[5]

Chapter 1 opens the book with a discussion about the various Bible translations. In chapter 2 we will look at the difference between the meaning of a passage and its significance to us individually. We also consider in chapter 2 the role that the Holy Spirit plays in the interpretive process. Chapters 3 through

---

[5] Do you get frustrated when books have endnotes in the back that you have to keep flipping to? I do. If you're reading this footnote, chances are, you're a footnote reader like me. I prefer to have them on the page I'm reading. So that's what you'll see in this book. Also, I often find myself wanting to include more detail, but to avoid making this book too long, or too academic, I make hefty use of the footnote. Feel free to ignore them if the content of the main text in the book suits your needs, but if you find yourself wanting to get more out of this study, I'd encourage you to read through them. So if you want that "textiness," you can find a lot of it in the footnotes.

7 introduce five principles for learning to interpret the Bible. Each chapter contains a verse that is a "sacred cow." Finally, in chapter 8 we will put the principles we have discussed into practice by looking at one last "sacred cow" as an example of the whole interpretive process.

Acts 17:11 (NIV) says "the Berean Jews were of more noble character than those in Thessalonica, for they received the message with great eagerness and examined the Scriptures every day to see if what Paul said was true." In that spirit, together let's examine the Scriptures.

Chapter 1

Which Bible?

Which translation of the Bible do you use? Years ago I was visiting my aunt while traveling on business. After a long day of work, I was quietly sitting down on her couch reading my Bible when she noticed the cover which read "NASB." She got a really funny look on her face and inquired, "What's that you're reading?" I told her it was my Bible. She seemed a bit perplexed and asked what NASB was. I replied, "Oh, it's the New American Standard Bible." She gasped in shock, and cried, "You mean you don't read the *Holy* Bible!?"

Obviously my aunt was no translation expert. She wasn't saying the NASB was a bad translation. In fact, as I discovered, she didn't even know there was more than one English version of the Bible. She had been raised always using the same translation of the Bible and the cover of hers simply read "Holy Bible." So when she saw me reading what she thought was another Bible, she was worried about my salvation and freaked out a little. We had a good laugh and I took the opportunity to talk to her about some different versions, including the one she used.

There are many translations of the Bible into English, so how do we choose which one is best for us? Are they all ok to use? There certainly are pros and cons for each translation, but before we get into some of the more significant differences, we need to clear up a couple misconceptions about Bible translation: one from outside the Christian community and one from inside.

Misconceptions About Bible Translation

A criticism that often comes from outside the Christian community goes something like this: "The Bible has been translated over and over so many times, how can we trust what we read?" The assumption here is that Bible translation is like the kids game "telephone," where one person starts with a phrase at one end of a line of kids and the expression winds up totally different at the other end. What starts as "I have to fix the hole in my shoe" winds up as "I once tripped in a whole pile of poo." More often than not, I suspect kids change it on purpose to get a laugh – I know because I was one of the ones who did. Some people see this analogy to be like the translation history of the Bible, suggesting that there has been a buildup of errors over time. But is it?

Unlike what this criticism suggests, this isn't the way that we get our translations of the Bible! Our translations have not been translated from Greek into Latin, from Latin into German, from German into Old English, and then into today's modern English translations. On the contrary, the English translations we use have been translated directly from the oldest and most reliable manuscripts of the Old and New Testament we have.[1] Each time a new translation is undertaken, the translators go back to the ancient documents to translate the Hebrew, Greek or Aramaic (the original languages the books of the Bible were written in) into the current language.

You may be thinking that I noted the oldest and most reliable manuscripts, and not the originals. The fact is we don't have the originals.[2] So what about the period of time from the originals to the oldest manuscripts we do have? Isn't that like the game of telephone? Sorry to burst your bubble, but it's not either. As we noted, in the game of telephone, kids often make a change on purpose just to be funny. But for the scribes who translated the Bible, messing up the original was no laughing matter.[3] The copying process was loaded with rules and procedures which they meticulously followed. Scribes were not allowed to write from memory, but had to copy from another manuscript. If errors were found, the page was systematically destroyed and redone.[4] Some scribes even believed that if they

---

1 For recent information on manuscript counts and reliability, see Jones, Clay. "The Bibliographical Test Updated." *CRI*. CRI, n.d. Web. 02 Nov. 2013. <http://www.equip.org/articles/the-bibliographical-test-updated/>.

2 God may have good reason for us not having the originals. Imagine if we did have the actual manuscripts. Would we begin to turn our awe and worship to them? Worship of relics has been common in church history. Would we value one book of the Bible over others if we had only that one? Many justifiable reasons can be thought of. Instead, God has provided us His Word, in the best possible way.

3 On occasion, a scribe may have made deliberate changes to the text to clarify something, replace a lost story, or even possibly to add to answer a theological dispute. A possible example occurs in 1 John 5:7-8. Most scholars agree that the portion "in heaven, the Father, the Word, and the Holy Ghost: and these three are one. And there are three that bear witness in earth" (KJV) is a 3rd of 4th century addition by a scribe (or scribes) to support the arguments for the Trinity which were reaching the final stages of development at that time. The small number of occasions where this may have occurred does not affect any major doctrine and is not considered by conservative scholars as reason to doubt the vast majority of the text.

4 For a basic introduction see Wegner, Paul D. "The Reliability of the Old Testament Manuscripts." *Understanding Scripture: An Overview of the Bible's Origin,*

messed up the copy, they would go to hell! While that certainly was bad theology, you can bet it made them extremely motivated and accurate copiers. This is strong evidence that there was little opportunity for errors to enter the text.

We can also have confidence in the oldest copies we have today because the original manuscripts were not copied in a straight line, one to another. Instead of telephone, we can think of the Bible copies more like the outgrowth of a bush or a tree, from which a single root (the original manuscript) produced many branches (ancient copies).

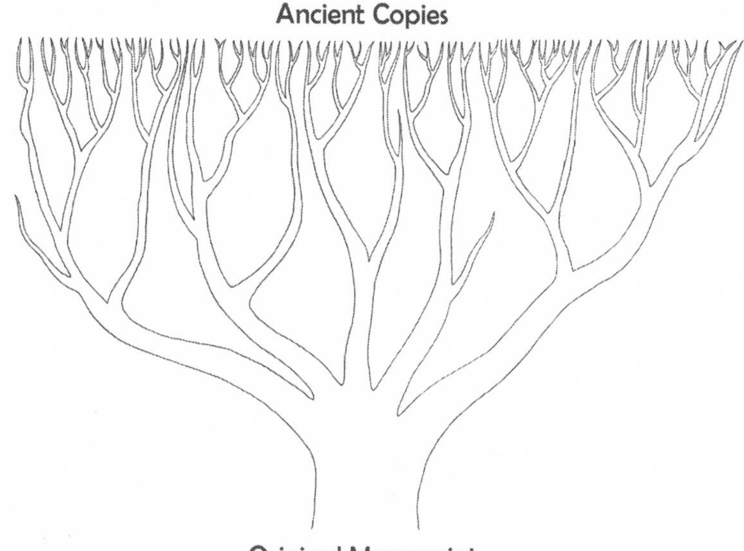

Reliability, and Meaning. Ed. Wayne A. Grudem, C. John Collins, and Thomas R. Schreiner. Wheaton, IL: Crossway, 2012. 101-09. Print. For a more thorough treatment see Wegner, Paul D. *A Student's Guide to Textual Criticism of the Bible: [its History, Methods & Results]*. Downers Grove, IL: IVP Academic/InterVarsity, 2006. Print.

What we have in our possession is thousands of ancient copies in the original language which all overwhelmingly agree. Considering the New Testament for example, we have over 5000 ancient original language copies to examine. And when there happens to be a variant, it's not anything that is of doctrinal significance. It's usually something like a number, or the spelling of a name.[5] That's nothing like the game of telephone. So, when we read a modern version of the Bible, what we have in our hands is an accurate rendering of the original, not a "game-of-telephone" translation.

There's another misconception that we may sometimes encounter. This one occurs inside the Christian community. I once observed this happen in a small Sunday school class. The person teaching the group referenced a commentary because there had been some dispute about the passage the week before. One of the people in the class, Jim, didn't like the fact that the teacher had used a commentary for assisting him in interpreting the Word of God. His objection was that as soon as the teacher put down his Bible and looked at commentaries, he was not relying on or trusting in God. Jim argued that we should read the Bible only and allow God to do *all* the interpreting.

The role of the Holy Spirit in the interpretive process will be discussed in more detail in Chapter 2, but for now it's important to note that there was a more fundamental mistake that Jim was making. What he didn't realize was that in his English translation of the Bible, there had already been some interpreting done for him. In fact, all translation is interpretation. Words from one language often don't correspond exactly to words in another, grammar is different, sentence structure doesn't match, and so

---

[5] There are a few passages which are in dispute, including John 7:53-8:11 and the ending of the Gospel of Mark (16:9-20). See footnote 3.

on. We need to realize that any time we use a translation we are relying on someone else to interpret the original work for us. This doesn't make a translation a commentary, but we need to acknowledge that with all translation there is interpretation decision-making inherent in the translated text.

The above examples represent two opposite extremes. In the first misconception, the individual believes that a translation is less than it actually is. In the second, the person thinks a translation is more than it actually is. When we read an English version of the Bible, we need to understand that a translation is both an accurate representation of the original, and yet not exactly the original, but rather an interpretation of the original.

The Purpose of Bible Translation

"If English was good enough for Jesus, it's dang well good enough for me" – Redneck Proverb

The Bible was primarily written in Hebrew (for the Old Testament) and Greek (for the New), with a few portions in Aramaic. In the U.S., we're lucky if we've learned one foreign language, let alone two or three. So how can we read the Word of God? We either need to learn these languages, or we need someone to translate it into English. The vast majority of us opt for a translation as opposed to spending years in school, but it comes with the sacrifice that we are leaving some of the interpretive process in the hands of translators. This is why we should, at a minimum, investigate the different translations that are available to us. We need to discover the pros and cons of each, and decide which translation is best for our situation.

Translations are sometimes written with a particular audience in mind. For example, there are several versions of children's

Bibles. There are also a few translations that purposely use a limited number of English words that are for people who might have difficulty with the English language. There's even a translation written specifically for people who love Shakespeare – it's called the King James Version. Ok, I'm kidding about that part, but it does bring up the question, why are some translations so much easier to read than others? In the case of the King James Version, a major reason it is so difficult to read is that it was written in 1611 and we no longer say "thee," "thine," "howbeit" and "doest" (except in Thor movies). But if we compare the New King James Version (NKJV) updated in 1982, to the God's Word translation (GW) completed in 1995, we still find a lot of differences. So why are *they* so different?

Different Approaches to Bible Translation

The goal of Bible translation is to help the modern reader enter into the ancient world of the text by translating the source language of the original into the receptor language of the reader. In simpler terms, the translator's aim is to take the message that the author meant to tell his first readers and make it understandable to us, in our language. If this is the goal of all translators, then why are there differences in translations? The answer is that there are two different schools of thought in Bible translation.

At one end of the spectrum, there are translations which put more emphasis on producing a word-for-word translation of the original. This approach attempts to preserve as much as possible the grammar and structure of the source. Scholars call this "formal equivalence." At the other end, the emphasis is placed on a thought-for-thought conversion. The intention here is to relay the overall idea or thought expressed in the original. Scholars label this approach "functional equivalence."

Some Challenges of Translation

If you've ever studied a foreign language, then you have some idea of the difficulties Bible translators face. Often there are words which just don't transfer well from one language to another – words which give precise meaning in one language but have no equivalent in another. There may be words in the receptor language which capture only part of the meaning of the original, so translators have to add to the translation to clarify the meaning. Sometimes it may be the opposite where the best word in the receptor language carries more meaning than the source, so again clarification may be needed.

Another problem that arises is the change of the meaning of words in the receptor language. Sometimes a word which had one meaning 20 or 30 years ago, may have an entirely different meaning today. For example the word "alien" in the 1984 New International Version (NIV '84) has been updated to "foreigner" in the NIV 2011. The translators note "who would have guessed in the 1970s that, within a few decades, an 'alien' would mean, thanks to the influence of ET and other movies and TV shows, an 'extraterrestrial being'?"[6] Along the same line of reasoning, it's not hard to figure out why the New American Bible (NAB) recently changed "booty" to "spoils of war." After all, the words of 2 Chronicles 28:15 ("All of them who were naked they

6 The Committee on Bible Translation. "Updating the New International Version of the Bible: Notes from the Committee on Bible Translation." N.p., Aug. 2010. Web. 20 Feb. 2011. <http://www.niv-cbt.org/niv-2011-overview/translators-notes/>.

clothed from the booty") could take on an entirely different meaning today.

As we can see, it's often difficult to find the right word in translation, and even then, the meanings of words change over time. This illustrates why word study is such an important part of Biblical interpretation and will be discussed in detail in chapter 7. But the challenge is not just in choosing words; translation is more than word choice.

From one language to another, there are differences in grammar, style and structure. Even if you don't speak French, you may be familiar with the phrase "Je t'aime." It's translated, "I love you." But if you were to translate it with a strict formal equivalence, it would be "I you love" because the sentence structure in French is sometimes different than in English. Bible translators face this difficulty as well.

Take for example the widely quoted verse, John 3:16. A strictly word-for-word translation of it would read "Thus indeed loved God the world that the Son the only begotten he gave that everyone who believes on him not might perish but might have life eternal."[7] This would be incredibly difficult to read in English if a translation was like this, so even one of the most formal translations, the New American Standard Bible (NASB), translates this passage as "For God so loved the world, that He gave His only begotten Son, that whoever believes in Him shall not perish, but have eternal life." But for some, the words "only begotten" may not make much sense. And others might wonder if "perish" means when a person physically dies. That's why the New Century Version (NCV), a more functional translation,

---

[7] "John 3:16 Biblos Interlinear Bible." *John 3:16 Biblos Interlinear Bible.* Helps Ministries, n.d. Web. 09 Apr. 2013. <http://interlinearbible.org/john/3-16.htm>. Note also that Hebrew is written from right to left.

renders it "God loved the world so much that he gave his one and only Son so that whoever believes in him may not be lost, but have eternal life." The NASB attempts to capture the original meaning of each word while adjusting the structure a bit for the reader to understand, while the NCV attempts to get the meaning of the passage to the reader in simple, readable, modern English.[8]

Formal or Functional?

So which approach is better: formal or functional? While no translation is purely formal or purely functional, there are many arguments favoring one approach over the other. Entire books have been written on Bible translation for those who wish to study this in greater detail, but here are just a few brief points that illustrate some difficulties with each approach.

Formal translations best capture the original wording, but can feel rigid and sound awkward. On the other hand, more functional translations arguably help more people to understand the message, but may leave out some of the richness in certain theological terms. An example is John 17:17 which in the NASB reads "Sanctify them in the truth; Your word is truth." In the New Living Translation (NLT), the verse is rendered "Make them holy by your truth; teach them your word, which is truth." The person new to the Bible will likely not fully comprehend the meaning of "Sanctify" in the NASB, and would understand the concept better initially by reading the NLT's "make them holy." Yet this rendering leaves out much of the fullness behind what sanctify means. More than just making one holy, to sanctify is to

---

[8] Every time I hear those two words "modern English" together, I so want to start busting out "I Melt with You." (If you didn't experience the 80s new wave music movement, this probably went right over your head. You missed out, sorry.)

set something apart for a special religious purpose. In this passage, Jesus is not just crying out to God to "make them holy," He is asking the Father to set the disciples apart from the world (similar to priests in the Old Testament[9]) so that they may be dedicated to God's service.[10] The reader who is more familiar with Biblical terms and reads a formal translation will have a fuller understanding of the meaning of this passage. So, there seems to be merit for both approaches.

Idioms represent perhaps the best way to show how one method of translation might be preferred over another. An idiom is "an expression of a given language that is peculiar to itself grammatically or cannot be understood from the individual meanings of its elements."[11] An example of an English idiom is: "Kill two birds with one stone." The point has nothing to do with birds or stones, but means "to accomplish two tasks with one action."

To understand the difficulty that translators face, imagine you had to translate the following: "People, hold your horses. It's a piece of cake." A completely formal approach to translating this might be: "Everyone, grab on to your stallion. It's a portion of dessert." Perhaps this might be appetizing to some with odd dietary choices, but most people are going to totally be disgusted with the idea of feeding on Mr. Ed, and they will miss the actual meaning of the statement which is "Everyone slow down. It's easy."

The Bible often uses idioms to communicate a point. Look at Psalm 12:2 for example. Young's Literal Translation (YLT),

---

[9] Exodus 28:41

[10] Bock, Darrell L. *Jesus According to Scripture: Restoring the Portrait from the Gospels.* Grand Rapids, MI: Baker Academic, 2002. 519-25. Print.

[11] "idiom." *The American Heritage Dictionary of the English Language*, Fourth Edition. 2003. Boston: Houghton Mifflin Company, 2003. Web. 13 Feb. 2011.

which takes a very formal approach says, "Vanity they speak each with his neighbour, Lip of flattery! With heart and heart they speak." The expression "heart and heart" is a Hebrew idiom which means something like "deceitfully," but to someone picking up and reading a more formal translation that expression is probably lost. The God's Word Translation (GW), which follows a much more functional approach, renders it "All people speak foolishly. They speak with flattering lips. They say one thing but mean another." The GW translation is not at all a word-for-word translation, but it captures the intended meaning of the text perhaps even better than the more formal translations.

Alternatively, there is certainly benefit from diving into the ancient world to discover the meaning of an idiom. Looking deeper into the text helps us cross the bridge of time and culture and enter into the world where the text was written. This is the value of the formal approach. It leaves more of the interpretive process to us, forcing us to learn more about the background and culture. When we do this we are better able to understand the meaning of the text, and gain a deeper knowledge of the Bible.

It could also be argued that the names of people groups and cities are not changed in even the most functional translations. Knowledge of the geography and cultural history requires some background research to fully comprehend and appreciate a text, so why not require that same research of idioms? Why make one part of the translation easy, while leaving some parts difficult? Again, Bible translation is not a simple process and both approaches discussed here have their merits.

The Various Translations

"What translation is best for me?" – average person to clerk at the book store

"You need this leather bound, gold-fringed, engraved, nickel plated tabbed version" – salesman

So, which one should you use? The following sections list the pros and cons of the different approaches to translation, along with some examples of each and reasons you might want to choose one over the other for a given purpose. As I noted before, Bible translations don't follow a 100% formal or functional approach, but rather lie somewhere on a spectrum. For that reason, I have also added an additional section entitled "In the Middle," which is just that: translations that are somewhere between formal and functional equivalence.

Formal Equivalence Translations

Examples: YLT, ESV, ASV, RSV, KJV, NKJV, NASB[12]
Pros: These translations are the truest to the original language, often capturing the ancient cultural elements more faithfully.

---

[12] You may be thinking, if the NKJV and the NASB are both formal equivalents, how come there's so much disagreement? It's easy to see why two paraphrases might disagree, but what about two formal translations? Why do they disagree? First, there is some range even in the formal translations where some are more formal than others. Another big reason is that there are different source texts. As noted, there are some discrepancies in the oldest copies we have. In some cases we might have 50 copies of a passage which word it one way, but we might have a slightly different version of that passage from a manuscript that is 300 years older. So which would you use, the oldest one, or the one we have more copies of? Arguments can be made for both sides, and thus we have occasions where even formal equivalents find disagreement. One chooses the oldest copy to source from; the other translation uses the source with the most manuscripts. Don't worry though, once again, no major doctrines are involved.

Cons: They are sometimes difficult or awkward to read. They contain idioms, metaphors or even words that don't make sense to the modern reader.

Best used for: Bible study.[13] General use once you're more comfortable with theological terms.

In the Middle

Examples: NIV, NET[14], HCSB, CEB, NJB

Pros: Translations toward the center of the spectrum offer a good middle ground by accurately representing the meaning of the original language, while generally remaining clear to modern readers.

Cons: Moving away from the formal translations means that there is more interpretation which can result in more faults in the translation, as well as the theology of the translators beginning to creep into the translation.

Best used for: General use. Great for the times you only have one translation available. This is the Bible you'll probably want with you on camping trips, days at the beach, reading in the garden, at the coffee shop, etc.

---

13 When you sit down for a Bible study, it is a good idea to have multiple translations available to you, and sometimes those translations may be from one of the other groups, but it is always recommended to have at least one Bible translation that fits in the formal equivalence category whenever you engage in serious Bible study.

14 The text of the NET translation is considered more functional but has extensive translation notes available to the reader. As the preface states, "the translators and editors used the notes to give a translation that was formally equivalent, while placing a somewhat more functionally equivalent translation in the text itself to promote better readability and understandability. The longstanding tension between these two different approaches to Bible translation has thus been fundamentally solved.". Accessed at http://www.netbible.com/content/net-bible-preface on July 15, 2012.

Functional Equivalence Translations

Examples: NLT, NCV, GNT, GW, NIrV
Pros: These translations are very easy to read. They feel natural, almost like a novel. They often feel more personal.
Cons: Even more interpretation results in greater potential of the translator adding content to or removing content from the original, and more theology of the translators starts coming through in the text. Key meanings and tone from the original language are sometimes lost.
Best used for: Reading large portions of the Bible at a single sitting. A Children's Bible. People brand new to the Bible. People for whom English is not their primary language.

Other Versions

Another type of Bible that you may encounter is a paraphrase. However, it's important to note that a paraphrase really isn't a translation. Instead of being translated from the original, it is a rewording, or an extended wording of a translation already in English. Therefore, paraphrases are much more like a commentary and should be considered as such. A couple examples are: The Living Bible (TLB) which is a rewording of the American Standard Version (ASV) made for children; and The Amplified Bible (AMP), also a rewording of the ASV, but intended to convey a fuller meaning of the original to English readers.

Some paraphrases, including The Living Bible, often go beyond translating the original text to the modern reader, and actually change the text to fit the world today. Psalm 119:105 (TLB) for example reads "Your words are a flashlight to light the path ahead of me." Did that just say that the Hebrews had batteries? The difficulty with these paraphrases is that background and cultural significance are not only lost, they are recast as modern fictions. Thus the original intended meaning can be more easily misunderstood.

One version of the Scriptures that has gained popularity since its release is *The Message* by Eugene Peterson. While technically a translation (as Peterson translated the text directly from the original languages), *The Message* reads much more like a paraphrase, to the point of being similar to a devotional commentary. Many people, including myself, have benefited from the richness of Peterson's translation.[15] Still, it's important to remember that it lies on the far end of functional equivalence and it lacks the benefit of having a consensus of translators.

While many Christians have found that paraphrases can be a blessing in those times when reading the Bible feels dry and a fresh perspective is needed, paraphrases should not be used for interpreting or discovering meaning in specific passages of the text.

Conclusion

While the Bible translation you choose may not be in the same category as deciding who you should marry or if you should have children, it is far more significant than choosing which television or phone to buy. Unfortunately, most of us probably spend more time researching our electronics than our Bible translation. Hopefully after reading this you can appreciate how important using the right translation actually is. So go do some research, pray about it and if you need to, get a new translation of the

---

[15] I often use *The Message* when I start studying a book. Before reading the book in depth, I start by reading through the entire book in *The Message*. I find it to be one of the most engaging introductions to studying books of the Bible.

Bible. The one you choose will shape the way you talk about and even think about God. And that's a big deal.

Questions

1. What are the two misconceptions about Bible translations and how would you answer someone who raised them as concerns?

2. Why is all translation interpretation?

3. What's the difference between formal and functional Bible translations?

4. What's the shortest verse in the English Bible? Is it John 11:35 "Jesus Wept"? Are you sure? Check out Job 3:2 in some different translations. Why do you suppose this is?

5. Take a look at 2 Samuel 18:25 in some formal and functional translations. Discuss why there is a difference. What is the benefit to translating the meaning of an idiom? What is the benefit to leaving the original idiom in the translation?

6. How do you think the translation you choose could impact your understanding of God?

7. What Bible translation do you think is best for you?

Chapter 2

What Does it Mean (to me)?[1]

There's a debate taking place over how we should read and apply the Bible. At the academic level, the debate is typically between conservative Christian scholars and more postmodern liberal scholars (who sometimes are only Christian in the sense that they would say they identify with the tradition, but don't necessarily believe it to be true). In many cases, potentially harmful aspects of the postmodern ideas have penetrated all the way down into small group Bible studies at traditional churches. At issue is how we understand and apply a book that is 2000 years old. Do we bring our world today (our personal experiences and contexts) along with us into the pages of Bible as we attempt to find its meaning? Or, do we look to the past

---

1 Many readers will find the content of this chapter to be the most challenging material in the book. So, if you want to take some time to let it digest (or if you just prefer shorter chapters), I recommend that you split this chapter into three segments. For part 1, read from the beginning through the section titled "What the Bible Says About Discerning Meaning." For part 2, read the section "Discovering the Meaning" through "Bible Play-by-Play." For the final segment, begin at the section titled "The Holy Spirit's Role in Discovering Meaning and Significance" and read through the end of the chapter. Also, if you happen to be doing this as a small group study, I would strongly consider taking this approach and spreading this chapter out over two or three meetings.

and try to understand the Bible in its original context? In other words, is it the responsibility of modern Christians to listen to new messages from God in our experiences, and then add to or change our understanding of the Word (as one scholar recently suggested),[2] or is the Bible a treasure whose everlasting truths should be guarded lest they be distorted (to paraphrase another)?[3]

Whose Words Are They Anyway?[4]

An iconic scene in the 1989 movie *Say Anything* has John Cusack holding a boom box over his head serenading Diane, the girl he loves. The song he blasts through her open window is Peter Gabriel's "In Your Eyes." His character, Lloyd, feels lost without Diane and believes he needs her love to be complete. With the touching lyrics and the dramatic impact in the film, many of its viewers have come to connect that song to their own personal love stories. Some have even duplicated the scene with both humorous and serious intentions.[5]

The song's lyrics tell of someone being lost and empty and wanting to run away, but then recognizing that they are only

---

[2] This comes from comments made by Rev. Harry Knox, minister in the United Church of Christ. Comments were from an interview with Robert P. Jones and described in his book: Jones, Robert P. *Progressive & Religious: How Christian, Jewish, Muslim, and Buddhist Leaders Are Moving beyond the Culture Wars and Transforming American Life.* Lanham, MD: Rowman & Littlefield, 2008. 88-90. Print.

[3] This other scholar would be the Apostle Paul. See the Scripture references below.

[4] Much of my thinking in this section I owe to DuVall and Hayes. I highly recommend chapters 10-13 in their textbook *Grasping God's Word.* Duvall, J. Scott., and J. Daniel Hays. *Grasping God's Word: A Hands-on Approach to Reading, Interpreting, and Applying the Bible.* Grand Rapids, MI: Zondervan, 2005. Print.

[5] Search Youtube for some reproductions that people have recorded.

complete when they are with the person that loves them.[6] While many see the song's words as describing a relationship between two people, a number of Christian artists (including Nicole Nordeman and the band The Wrecking) have covered the song with a different twist. For them, the song is a hymn to God. Like many of us who are at times dishonest, selfish or prideful, and in those moments we run from God, the words of the song seen in this way describe the repentant believer removing their façade, swallowing their pride, and returning to God's love. One set of words; two different meanings.

Here's a different collection of words:

> "The driver of any vehicle approaching a stop sign at the entrance to, or within, an intersection shall stop at a limit line, if marked, otherwise before entering the crosswalk on the near side of the intersection." [7]

This sentence comes straight out of the California Vehicle Code. Unless you're looking for a ticket to add to your growing collection, you better only get one meaning from this set of words. The police officer and the judge sure won't have any problem determining the meaning. Of course, you could always follow the advice of my high school friend Robbie who said the white "O" around the stop sign stood for "optional." But be prepared to pay the consequences.

Two sets of words. In the first, different individuals can get different meanings from the words, and it's ok. In the second, you would be wise to know the actual meaning the author(s)

---

[6]Because of the ridiculously strict copyright laws on song lyrics, you'll have to go to the internet if you want to read the lyrics to the song. AZ Lyrics is one website that has lyrics available. See: www.azlyrics.com/lyrics/petergabriel/inyoureyes.html.

[7] "V C Section 22450 Stop Requirements." *V C Section 22450 Stop Requirements.* N.p., n.d. Web. 02 Sept. 2012. <http://dmv.ca.gov/pubs/vctop/d11/vc22450.htm>.

intended. This is a critical point to consider when we approach any written form of communication. Sometimes the author's intended meaning doesn't seem to matter. We make it mean what we want. Other times getting the wrong meaning can lead to unfortunate consequences (as in the case of a traffic ticket). So, is there a right way and a wrong way to interpret meaning from someone else's words? Yes… and no.

Did that confuse you enough? If not, try reading some books on literary analysis. Authors have written boatloads of material about where the meaning of a text is found. They use big terms like deconstructionism, structuralism and reader-response.[8] Not to minimize the significance of those discussions, but the simple fact is that how you determine the meaning of a text ultimately boils down to one basic question:

Do you care what the author is trying to communicate?

If you're concerned with the author's message, then like the traffic laws, there is only one meaning – a meaning the author intended, which you as the reader are trying to discover. If you don't really care about what the author is trying to communicate and you are purely enjoying the material for its aesthetic value, then you can make it mean whatever you want it to mean. You, the author and everyone else are none the worse for wear.

---

[8] One of the most ridiculous assertions that many reader-response advocates make is to suggest that you can't really get at, or know, an author's intended meaning. They argue for pages and pages, how that it's not possible to discover what an author's intention was. But do you see the total irony in this? These reader-response advocates fully expect that you can understand their point! That's why they wrote the book. But that's just silly. It's like saying "Reasons can't help you win an argument, and here's why." Or "My biological brother is an only child." It's self-refuting. So, if you ever hear someone trying to suggest that you can't really ever understand an author's intended meaning, just tell them that you interpret their statement to mean that you can. They'll have no way to respond. (If you don't get that, just think about it for a minute.)

Can the Bible Mean Anything We Want It To?

So which of these is the Bible like? Can we get multiple meanings from the same sets of words in Scripture? If you're just looking at the Bible as literature, as if it was only a piece of art, then what difference would it make if it meant one thing to you and another thing to someone else? Absolutely none. Who cares? It's just an opinion of how one person sees the book, and your opinion of it artistically is just as valid as anyone else's opinion. So if the Bible is *only* a piece of literature, then it can have whatever meaning the reader wants it to be *for them.*

However, as Christians, when we consider the Bible's primary author,[9] we're talking about the Ultimate Being, the Creator of the universe, and the Master of language – our God. And we certainly care what message He is communicating to us. As theologian D.A. Carson puts it "We are dealing with God's thoughts: we are obligated to take the greatest pains to understand them truly and to explain them clearly."[10]

Meaning and Significance

Right about now some of us might be thinking "But when I read the Bible, it means something special to *me.*" You may have a verse or passage of Scripture where God delivered something special to your heart as you read it; perhaps an encouraging

---

9 God did choose certain people, in certain cultures and certain circumstances to write specific things, and their personal elements are clearly embedded in the Scriptures. Still, He is the ultimate author of the Bible. He intended to communicate His message to us using the people He chose through the influence of the Holy Spirit. If we care what message God is trying to communicate, then we realize that the meaning He intended and transferred to parchment through the human authors, is the only meaning there is or ever will be and that meaning is the same meaning for all His people.

10 Carson, D. A. *Exegetical Fallacies.* Grand Rapids, MI: Baker Book House, 1984. 15. Print.

whisper or a convicting cry. The Word of God is powerful that way, and the Holy Spirit works in us to help us draw personal application from the Word.

It's critical at this point that we recognize the distinction between the *meaning* of a text and its *significance.* Meaning is what the author is trying to convey to the reader. It is *discovered* by the reader, not *created* by him. It's already there in the text before the reader arrives. Significance is how the text affects or applies to the reader. It is personal. Significance is the impact a text has upon the individual after they've read it.

Unfortunately, all of us have been influenced by a culture which teaches us to value self-importance over truth. This causes us to look to our individual concern before we consider an author's point. We no longer ask the two part question "What does the passage mean? And how is that significant to me?" Instead we have opted for the single question "What does the passage mean to me?" as if its meaning were somehow dependent on the person reading it. But again, since we care what message the author is trying to communicate, we need to remember that the meaning of the text is the same for all readers.[11] Significance is what we get from the text that is personal.

---

[11] For some passages of Scripture, discovering the meaning can be very difficult. Sometimes there are passages which good Christians disagree on the meaning. However, just because there's disagreement about a passage's meaning doesn't mean there isn't a correct one. To borrow an analogy I've heard from Frank Beckwith, "Just because at one time people disagreed whether the earth was flat or round didn't mean it didn't have any shape." We should continue to be diligent, dialogue and study the word to understand the message God is communicating.

What the Bible Says About Discerning Meaning

Below are a few passages *from* God's word *about* God's word that we can reflect on. The first few come from the book of 2 Timothy. This is particularly significant because it was the last thing in the Bible that the Apostle Paul wrote. The letter was written to his disciple Timothy when Paul knew he was about to be executed. If you were about to die and were writing a final letter to your protégé, don't you think you would include some of the things that you thought would be significant for him or her to know about carrying on your work?[12]

> "All Scripture is God-breathed and is useful for teaching, rebuking, correcting and training in righteousness, so that the servant of God may be thoroughly equipped for every good work." 2 Timothy 3:16-17 (NIV)

The Bible is inspired by God and is for us to learn from so that we may do the good works God desires of us.

It is important to note here that the Greek word for Scripture in this verse is *graphe,* which means the writings. It is the words that are inspired.[13] Sometimes people mistake this passage as teaching that the meaning or the significance the person gets from it is inspired, but that is certainly not what is being taught here by Paul. It is the words.

Also of note is the term "God-breathed" in the NIV. The actual Greek word is *theopneustos,* the second part of which is

---

12 This selection of verses and some of the comments that follow them come from listening to numerous podcasts and lectures by Greg Koukl of Stand to Reason. See their website at www.str.org

13 The words are what are inspired, but God also clearly chose to place them in their grammatical, literary and historical context.

related to Greek word for Spirit.[14] The Holy Spirit inspired the human authors as they wrote the text. It is God-breathed; His words; His meaning. As popular writer Kay Arthur notes "When we ascribe meaning to a passage that the author did not intend, then we are assuming an authority equivalent to that of the author. And the author of all Scripture is really God."[15]

Finally, note that the second half of the verse begins with "so that." There is a reason God inspired the words for us. We study the Bible and discover the meaning "so that" we may draw personal application from it. Therefore, ultimately, the purpose of discovering the correct meaning is "so that" we may be equipped for good works.[16]

> "Be diligent to present yourself approved to God as a workman who does not need to be ashamed, accurately handling the word of truth." 2 Timothy 2:15 (NASB)

Paul's words here teach that we are to do our best in our study to get the correct meaning from the Bible. Be diligent and get it right!

Additionally, it seems fair to say that if there is an accurate way to handle Scripture (as this verse states), then there is an

---

[14] This is the only time this word *theopneustos* appears in the Bible. Some think Paul invented the word by combining *theo* (God) with *pneumo* (breath or Spirit) to describe God's action of inspiring the Scriptures. As we will note in our chapter on word study, we need to be cautious when using etymology to determine word meaning. However, in this instance, the context clearly supports that this is indeed what Paul means by the term. For those that want to go even deeper into the discussion as to whether *theopneustos* is a predicate adjective or an attributive adjective, for an excellent overview see Knight, George W. *The Pastoral Epistles: A Commentary on the Greek Text.* Grand Rapids, MI: W.B. Eerdmans, 1992. 444-50. Print.

[15] Arthur, Kay. *How to Study Your Bible.* Eugene, Or.: Harvest House, 1995. 64. Print.

[16] McKnight, Scot. "The Boring Chapter (on Missional Listening)." *The Blue Parakeet: Rethinking How You Read the Bible.* Grand Rapids, MI: Zondervan, 2008. 104-12. Print.

inaccurate way as well. Therefore, we should be careful that we are accurately handling the Word of God. Finally, notice that this verse also tells us what using the Bible accurately depends on: our own diligent work.

> "Retain the standard of sound words which you have heard from me, in the faith and love which are in Christ Jesus. Guard, through the Holy Spirit who dwells in us, the treasure which has been entrusted to you." 2 Timothy 1:13-14 (NASB)

Here Paul is telling Timothy to protect the Bible. This is especially critical because Paul later mentions (in 4:3-4) that there will come a time when people will "not endure sound doctrine; but wanting to have their ears tickled, they will accumulate for themselves teachers in accordance to their own desires, and will turn away their ears from the truth and will turn aside to myths" (NASB). We need to protect Scripture from those who would distort it. This would include our own potential misinterpretations. We need to guard the treasure we have been entrusted with.

> "as also in all his letters, speaking in them of these things, in which are some things hard to understand, which the untaught and unstable distort, as they do also the rest of the Scriptures, to their own destruction." 2 Peter 3:16 (NASB)

This verse tells us that Scripture can be abused. Indeed, there are those that will distort the words of the Bible. In fact, this is exactly what the devil did to Christ during His temptation in the wilderness (Matt. 4:1-11). Satan tried to misuse Scripture passages to convince Jesus to act against the Father. He distorted

God's Word. And just as Jesus corrected Satan's misuse, we need to do our best to make sure we are interpreting the text correctly and to correct others who misuse it.

> "Rather, we have renounced secret and shameful ways; we do not use deception, nor do we distort the word of God. On the contrary, by setting forth the truth plainly we commend ourselves to everyone's conscience in the sight of God." 2 Corinthians 4:2 (NIV)

Again, do not distort the Bible. We need to learn the word, treat it responsibly and then share the truth.

Clearly the Bible teaches that there is one meaning.[17] If there were more than one meaning in the text, then why would the Bible tell us to be diligent, not distort and to retain the standard? If there's not a correct meaning, there's no reason to be diligent to find it. If there's not a correct meaning, then there's nothing to not distort. If there's not a correct meaning, then there's no reason to try to retain a standard, because there would be no standard.

It's evident from these passages that the human authors, under the inspiration of the Holy Spirit, believed that there is a correct meaning to the words of Scripture. It's our task today to pursue that meaning, and to protect it.

---

[17] By "one meaning" I mean that within a passage, there is only contained what the original author intended through the inspiration of the Holy Spirit. But in using the term "one" I do not wish to rule out a potential "fuller meaning" as a depth or extension of the meaning which may unfold as history passes. For example, some suggest the possibility of Old Testament prophecies containing typological meaning. *If* that is the case in a passage, then it certainly would be part of the intended meaning that the Holy Spirit thought to communicate. However, due to the scope of this book, there is insufficient space and time to cover advanced hermeneutical issues. I would recommended the reader to some of the textbooks referenced in the footnotes of this chapter.

Discovering the Meaning

How can we be confident we're on the right track and getting the correct meaning when we study Scripture? One of my favorite books on Bible interpretation says that it is "absolutely critical to understand as well as we possibly can what God means by what he says in the Bible. We must understand correctly so we can act correctly. There is no benefit to following – even with great and earnest sincerity – a mistaken point of view."[18] So how do we do discover "what God means by what he says in the Bible"?

Some things are just plain obvious. Like the familiar sign I see every time I drive from California to Arizona: "State Prison. Do not pick up Hitchhikers." Duh. Likewise, some passages of Scripture are pretty straightforward. For example, James 4:7 (NASB) "Submit therefore to God. Resist the devil and he will flee from you." Or John 15:12 (NASB) "This is My commandment, that you love one another, just as I have loved you." Others are more complex, such as 1 John 5:16 (NASB), "If anyone sees his brother committing a sin not leading to death, he shall ask and God will for him give life to those who commit sin not leading to death. There is a sin leading to death; I do not say that he should make request for this." Or Genesis 6:4 (NASB) "The Nephilim were on the earth in those days, and also afterward, when the sons of God came in to the daughters of men, and they bore children to them. Those were the mighty men who were of old, men of renown." Huh? What's a sin leading to death and a sin that doesn't? And what the heck are Nephilim? And who's having children with whom? This is more confusing than Bernie Madoff's tax return.

---

18 Klein, William W., Craig Blomberg, Robert L. Hubbard, and Kermit Allen Ecklebarger. *Introduction to Biblical Interpretation.* Dallas, TX: Word Pub., 1993. 18. Print.

Discovering the accurate meaning often involves many things, including considering the literary, historical and immediate context as well as understanding the key words in the passage and searching the Scriptures for what else the Bible teaches that is related to the passage. As we move through the rest of this book, we will cover each of those five topics, but there are a couple "big picture" interpretive guidelines we need to discuss first.

Descriptive / Prescriptive

The first big picture concept we need to understand is that there is a difference between descriptive and prescriptive writings. The Bible contains both types. What's the difference? In Acts 15:36-41 Paul and Barnabas have such a "sharp disagreement" over whom to take with them on their journey that they split up over it. Is there a lesson there? Is God telling us that if two people can't agree about how to spread the gospel that they should part ways? Or is this just a description of what happened and we shouldn't make anything of it?

Perhaps an analogy may help. One morning your teenage daughter wakes up with a fever, a headache, a painful sore throat and feels exceptionally tired. She's been dragging for a couple days now, so you make an appointment with her doctor. After a few tests, the doctor reveals that your daughter has something called mononucleosis, or "mono" for short. He describes the illness to you, explaining how the virus attacks her body and causes her symptoms. He points out that it has the nickname "kissing disease" because it is commonly spread among teens through the exchange of saliva. (You give your daughter the "we'll talk about that later" look.) Then to help with the fever and headaches, the doctor writes a prescription for a pain reliever. He also tells you to be sure that your daughter avoids any contact activities such as sports for several weeks due to the potential of a ruptured spleen associated with the virus.

Here's the point. Part of this visit with the doctor was him just describing the situation to you. He told you about the virus and how she may have picked it up. There's really no direct instruction to your daughter or you that needs to be followed. It's just the doctor explaining some things about the condition. Another part of the appointment is him prescribing the medicine to take and some behavior restrictions that should be followed. This is direct advice that you and your daughter should listen to.

The Bible is like this in some ways. A large part of the Scriptures, including the history contained in the Old Testament, is descriptive. We are reading accounts that describe what happened to God's people in *their* history. Alternatively, much of the Bible is also prescriptive. Paul's letters to the churches for example are filled with instruction that believers today ought to follow. The application of prescriptive information is usually quite simple. Do what it says. But like the analogy of the doctor's office, just because something is descriptive doesn't mean there isn't application. If you have a younger daughter, you could use her older sister's story of contracting mono as an example of why she shouldn't be kissing so many boys. There is a lesson learned from the example of her older sibling. In the same way, we can sometimes use the descriptive stories of the Bible to get valuable life lessons.

One obvious example of a descriptive account with an application we can learn comes from the book of Joshua. Faced with seemingly insurmountable walls around Jericho, the Israelites could have given up. Yet the Lord told Joshua to have his army march around the city for seven days (once a day for six days, then seven times on the seventh day) and the walls of the city would collapse. The people of Israel follow God's direction exactly. On the seventh day, the miraculous occurs! The walls collapse and God's people are victorious.

Now, does this story teach us a prescriptive lesson that if we want to capture a city with great walls surrounding it that we should march around the city in this manner? No, of course not. But we can learn other important lessons from this account. For one, we can see that God is faithful to fulfill His promises to His people when they follow His commands. To the Israelite army it may have seemed ridiculous to parade around the city for seven days instead of attacking it head on, but they trusted the Lord. They didn't stop after six days and say "This is stupid. Let's go back to camp." They knew God is a God who comes through on His promises. They had just spent forty years in the desert learning that lesson! We can have the same confidence today. When we read God's timeless promises in the Bible, we can know, as the Israelites did when they marched around Jericho, that God is a faithful God. He comes through on His promises, sometimes in some really cool ways.

While many stories from the Bible offer teaching points for today, not all descriptive accounts necessarily have something we can learn imbedded within them. Sometimes, like in the case of polygamy and concubines in the days of Solomon, it's just what happened. It doesn't mean that God has commanded or even approves of those actions. They are just recorded as part of the narrative. Sometimes they play a role in the story, but we should be careful not to read too much into them if the text itself is not tying them to the larger context of the story.[19]

---

[19] Still, be careful not to rule out application from descriptive accounts too quickly. There are plenty of "oughts" for today found in the Bible's descriptive

Finally, while much of the Old Testament is descriptive, and much of the New Testament is prescriptive, it is important to note that it's not just an Old Testament / New Testament thing. The Proverbs of the Old Testament offer us words of wisdom that we generally ought to follow. In some cases, they could be considered prescriptive. And likewise, the New Testament has plenty of descriptive accounts such as the one involving Paul and Barnabas noted above. The important thing is to figure out if what we are reading is descriptive or prescriptive. As we continue through this book, we will often return to this idea, especially in chapter 4 when we discuss the different types of writing found in the Bible.

Bible Play-by-Play

There are many tools that we can use to help enhance our Bible study. One of the main instruments widely available is Bible commentaries. They are just what their name suggests. Commentaries offer interpretations (or comments) on the Bible. They are generally simple to use and can be quite beneficial.[20]

I'm a sports fan and like to watch a lot of different sports, including baseball, but the experience of watching a baseball game is greatly enhanced when I've got Vin Scully (the broadcaster for the Los Angeles Dodgers) giving the play-by-play. His commentary adds so much to the experience. From the historical anecdotes that relate to the game, to the clarity

---

writings. Sometimes it just takes more study and prayer to see the lesson, or principle. We will have more to say about this in the chapter on genre.

20 A list of some recommended commentaries by category is provided in Appendix 1. If you use another commentary, be sure to learn a little about it first. Is it in a reputable series? What is the author's perspective? If you're not sure, run it by your pastor or someone you know that has some knowledge in the area.

provided on a confusing play, his observations make watching the game ten times better.

Reading commentaries when we're doing our Bible study is a lot like having Vin Scully with us at a baseball game. They provide historical background, explain the context, offer relevant applications, and more. Commentaries help us better understand (and in some cases just understand) the passage we're studying.

Fortunately, there are many varieties of Bible commentaries available. Whether you've been studying the Bible your whole life and are looking for a commentary that goes into details of the original language, or you're new to the Bible and looking for something that gives you just enough background to help you develop some solid applications, there's a commentary series out there for you.

If you're new to the Bible, then like someone watching a sport for the first time, you may want the commentary right there with you as you study. Others may prefer to use commentaries at the end of their Bible study so they're not automatically led in the direction the commentary goes. In this way, the commentary is used as a check system to make sure you're not misunderstanding or misapplying the text. This is the process I generally follow. However, I do use reference tools such as concordances and background notes (we'll discuss these later) at the very beginning of my Bible study because they often provide key information I need for proper interpretation. The basic information in those sources is helpful so I can more easily and accurately discover the meaning and find application from the text.

The Holy Spirit's Role in Discovering Meaning and Significance

The Holy Spirit is often the person of the Trinity that gets the least amount of our consideration.[21] We pray to the Father, sing to the Son, and remember the Spirit whenever we are reminded that the tri- in Trinity means three. Yet, when it comes to Christians promoting their view of a Bible passage, His name gets thrown around by us as if we were a little kid on the playground shouting "My dad says, __________(blah, blah, blah), and he's smarter than your dad!" I once heard a pastor who was teaching on the free will / predestination debate[22] say to the congregation that the Holy Spirit had spoken to him and told him that his interpretation, which happened to be the Arminian (free will) view, was the correct one. As if the teaching giants of the past including Calvin, Spurgeon and Edwards (all who taught the opposite view) didn't have as good of a line to God as this pastor did!

Why are we so quick to invoke the name of the Holy Spirit when we're talking about Bible interpretation? Are we being defensive because we haven't really done our homework? Do we see it as a short cut to just get others to trust us? After all, who's going to argue with someone who got their interpretation directly from God? But does the Holy Spirit actually "speak" the meaning to us? And what happens if He speaks a different, even opposite, meaning to someone else? We can't both be right, can we?

---

21 Please read *Forgotten God.* It's an amazing book about the Holy Spirit, and our relationship to Him. Chan, Francis, and Danae Yankoski. *Forgotten God: Reversing Our Tragic Neglect of the Holy Spirit.* Colorado Springs, CO: David C. Cook, 2009.

22 If you're not familiar with this topic, essentially it is the debate over how we become saved. Is it God or us? Though there is much, much more to it. For an excellent overview, see Correia, John P. *Refreshing Grace.* Phoenix: Biblical Framework, 2012.

One way we can better understand how the Holy Spirit works within us in the interpretive process is to compare a believer's reading of the Bible to a non-believer's. Could a person who doesn't believe the Bible is the Word of God still discover its meaning? In *A Basic Guide to Interpreting the Bible*, Robert Stein uses the example of two groups of college students, one Christian, the other not, who are given an assignment to write a paper on what Paul meant in a passage of the Bible. How would the students fare? Stein writes,

> "I would suggest that the curve of the grades of both groups, all other things being equal, would be quite similar. Non-Christians can arrive at a correct mental grasp of the meaning of the Bible…Otherwise why try to explain the Gospel message to them? Why would Paul reason every Sabbath in the synagogues (Acts 18:4)?"[23]

In other words, Paul told non-Christians about the Gospel message in the Scriptures. He read from the Word of God to non-believers. He wouldn't have done so if he thought non-Christians couldn't understand what the Scriptures meant. Paul knew they could understand what the Scriptures said, so he shared them with non-believers. It seems pretty clear that if any person, believer or not, follows good interpretive methods (including studying the language, culture, context, and so on), they will be able to reach an understanding of at least the basic meaning of the Bible, in the same way that they can understand any book.

---

[23] Stein, Robert H. *A Basic Guide to Interpreting the Bible: Playing by the Rules.* Grand Rapids, MI: Baker, 1999. 67. Print.

As an example, let's return to our discussion of Jericho. A non-believer can read the account, understand the events and get the sense of the story. Furthermore, if they're familiar with the Bible, then they would see how the story relates to the big picture of Israel's relationship to its God. A non-believer may even have a cognitive understanding of the beliefs that the Israelites held about their God. But reading the account and analyzing the fundamental elements of the meaning of the text is the extent of their experience.[24]

For the believer, here is where the process begins to get significantly different – and really awesome. The Holy Spirit indwells the believer (1 Cor. 3:16, 6:19; James 5:5; Rom. 8:9) so He is with the reader through this entire process. But not only is the Holy Spirit with the believer as he reads the text, He convinces the believer of the truth of the words as the believer reads (see John 15:26, Acts 5:32, Romans 8:16). So while a person without the Holy Spirit may be able to see from the outside the beliefs that followers of God have, what they don't know is what it's actually like to experience those beliefs. A non-believer can't relate to the Israelites victory at Jericho the way a Christian does. A non-believer, as an observer, sees what the story means to the people involved and how they are impacted – but they see it only from the outside. Without the Holy Spirit, they don't grasp what it means to one who is a follower of the

---

[24] A couple points here. One, the non-believer may have a different experience if they are not looking for the meaning in the sense we have been advocating it. If they are reading the text just as a piece of literature for the aesthetic value, they may come away with some subjective interpretation of the story's meaning. Additionally, a non-believer may think of some personal application, but it wouldn't be the same kind of experience for them. For example, a non-believer may read a Proverb and think to themselves, "That makes sense, I'm going to act in that way." However, it is likely for personal motivation, not with the intent to please God as one of His followers.

God whom the story is about.[25] In contrast, believers relate to the experience. They have the same feelings of comfort, hope and confidence as the Israelites had (though perhaps with different intensity).

Believers know God. R.A. Torrey writes,

> "No amount of listening to sermons and lectures, no matter how able, no amount of mere study of the Word even would ever give us to see 'the things of Christ'; the Holy Spirit must show us and He is willing to do it and He can do it…The Spirit reveals to the individual believer the deep things of God, things which human eye hath not seen, nor ear heard, things which have not entered into the heart of man, the things which God hath prepared for them that love Him."[26]

So, without the Holy Spirit a person gets the basic meaning, but they don't experience the fullness of the story, and they certainly don't draw the same kind of application that a believer draws from it.

More than just convincing us of the truth of the Bible, the Holy Spirit transforms us through it. You may have heard something like, "You don't just read the Bible; the Bible reads

---

[25] See 1 Corinthians 2:14. Some translations can be a bit confusing here because they use the word "understand." Paul is not saying that non-believers don't understand the message of the Bible in the sense that they are unable to comprehend the meaning of the words. What Paul *is* saying is that the non-believer *does* see what the text is saying, but that they reject it as foolishness. The non-believer doesn't have the Holy Spirit convincing them of the truth. Since the non-believer rejects the message, they are unable to "understand" the spiritual aspects of the meaning, and unable to find any significance from it. That's the point Paul is making in 1 Corinthians.

[26] Torrey, R. A. *The Person and Work of The Holy Spirit.* New York: Fleming H. Revell, 1910. 146-48. Print.

you." For Christians that's absolutely true! When we read the Bible, the words jump out of the page and into our soul, convicting us of our iniquity, and drawing us closer to God. Scripture teaches us what God desires of His people, and we are changed by what we learn. As we progress, we are made more and more like Christ. Theologians call this process progressive sanctification. The Holy Spirit uses the words He inspired in the Bible to transform us today. And it's the same way He has been doing it for the past 2000 years.

Lastly, it is important to note that the Holy Spirit does not "inspire" us in the sense that is used when someone describes the inspiration of the Bible writers. The original human authors were inspired by the Holy Spirit to write the words of the Bible (2 Timothy 3:16-17; John 14:26), but when the last Apostle died and Scripture was completed, that process was finished.[27] Nothing new has been added to the canon of Scripture.[28] What the Holy Spirit does for us today is "illuminate" the Scriptures by convincing us of their reality, revealing to us the "deep things of God" and transforming our souls.

---

27 For the theologians who are reading this, just for the record, I am not a cessationist. This is a canon issue.

28 The first time you hear someone say "Biblical canon," you might think it's something was developed to destroy the Bible. But the word is canon, not cannon. The term "canon" refers to the books that are considered inspired by God and included in the Bible. For an excellent introduction to canonicity, see Blue Letter Bible. - *Help, Tutorials, and FAQs.* N.p., n.d. Web. 20 Aug. 2012. <http://www.blueletterbible.org/faq/canon.cfm>.or Grudem, Wayne A. "The Canon of Scripture." *Systematic Theology: An Introduction to Biblical Doctrine.* Leicester, England: Inter-Varsity, 1994. 54-72. Print.

When we open the pages of Scripture and read, a rough description of the process that occurs might look like this:

(1) We discover the meaning of the text;[29]

(2) The Holy Spirit gives us the confidence that what we read is true;[30] and

(3) The Holy Spirit teaches us a personal application or significance from the Word. It is this last part of the process that most pointedly draws us to God and His will for us.

Significance: How Does It Apply To Me?

Let's look at 2 Timothy 3:16-17 again. Paul writes "All Scripture is God-breathed and is useful for teaching, rebuking, correcting and training in righteousness, so that the servant of God may be thoroughly equipped for every good work." As we noted above, the meaning of this passage of Scripture is that the Bible is inspired by God and is for us to use so that we may do the good works God desires of us. That's the meaning. The Holy Spirit assures us of this reality as we meditate on these words. But how is it significant for each believer? Certainly one application would be to study the Bible and have it be useful in your life.

---

[29] One question I haven't really addressed is, "Does the Spirit aid the believer in the process of discovering the meaning of the text?" Perhaps. He certainly is right there with the believer as he reads. But if non-believers can reason the same meaning, then what exactly is it that the Spirit is doing in this part of the process? I don't know that we can say for certain. Maybe since knowing the meaning is necessary for both non-believers (for salvation) and believers (for sanctification) the Holy Spirit is with both of them equally the same? On the other hand, maybe the Holy Spirit waits for us to put in the work and discover that meaning on our own? As we read in 2 Timothy 2:15, the Bible tells us that we are to be diligent and accurately handle the word of truth. That sounds like it could be our job. Either way, or perhaps a little of both, the one thing that is clear is that the Holy Spirit doesn't give different meanings to different people. There is only one unchanging meaning that the Holy Spirit had already inspired in the text before we ever got there.

[30] Just to clarify here, I mean true in the sense of absolute truth, not some relative "true for you" kind of belief.

Another person might use this passage and apply it to a different passage they are struggling with, giving them confidence even though they may not understand the other passage. They still know that all Scripture is God-Breathed. These are general applications that many people probably get from the passage. But what about specific personal applications? For example, say a college student is trying to decide between business school and pastoral ministry. After reading this passage and feeling led by the Holy Spirit, would a proper application be choosing to be a pastor and teaching the Word? What about another student deciding between architecture and law enforcement, specifically working at a correctional facility? If they feel led by the Spirit to choose working in the correctional system so that they can "correct and train in righteousness," is that a proper application that the Spirit really intended when He inspired this text?

As we discussed, there is one meaning to the text, but there can be multiple applications. Still, that doesn't mean that we can just get any application from any passage of Scripture. If that was the case, we might as well open up a book of Robert Frost poetry and ask the Spirit to teach us from it. The Bible is not just words that the Holy Spirit maneuvers to fit our circumstances depending upon what page we're on. Passages in the Bible have specific meaning for a reason. We go to it to discover God's truth and apply it to our lives.[31] It has power that way. But if we don't use the Bible the way God intended, we rob it of that power.

---

31 Just a quick note here. We often hear the phrase "apply the Bible to our lives" and I use it throughout this book. However, I really think a better way to think about it is to "apply our lives to the Bible." What that means is that we shouldn't be so focused on how God can get involved in ***our*** lives. Instead, we should be seeking how we can serve *Him*. But rather than go off topic and/or confuse the reader, I will stick with the more conventional language.

While each passage has a specific meaning, there is a range or pattern of meaning that we can consider when we look for application. For example, in Ephesians 5:18 Paul writes "Do not get drunk with wine." Paul's meaning here is pretty simple: drunkenness with wine is prohibited. However, within the scope of Paul's meaning, there are many other things which would apply.[32] For one, Paul's command here would certainly include beer as well, even though he doesn't specifically mention it. In fact, proper application of this passage would also include not getting "wasted" by smoking marijuana. Even though Paul wasn't aware of a drug, it still falls within the implication of what he wrote. The principle we get from the meaning in this verse is that we should not be putting substances in our bodies which alter our consciousness just for fun. There are several applications which can come out of that meaning depending on our individual circumstances.

Though applications are multifaceted and passages apply to different people in different ways, we still need to be careful not to go outside the scope of meaning. As a parent, I have regular conversations with my kids that can help illustrate this. One example I recall is my son playing video games on the Wii. For several days, he was enjoying a process my wife and I set up for him: do his homework and then get to play 30 minutes of Mario Kart, his favorite game at the time. Still, he would ask every day right when he got home. "Dad, can I play Mario Kart now?" "As soon as your homework is done," I would reply. One day I left the room for ten minutes. I came back, and he was playing Wii Sports! "Is your homework done?" I asked. "No," he sullenly answered. And because he knew he was in trouble, he added, "But you said I couldn't play Mario Kart. I'm playing Wii

---

[32] Stein, *A Basic Guide to Interpreting the Bible: Playing by the Rules*, 38-43.

Sports," his tone perking up as if he had just won some academic award. He thought perhaps I'd be impressed with his reasoning. Not so. He knew what I meant, and after we talked, he admitted it. He realized that he chose to twist my words because it got him what he desired. Kids look for little nuances to get outside of what their parents mean often because it suits their purpose. Is it possible that this behavior still comes out in us as adults? Even worse, do we sometimes do this with the Bible? Perhaps. So while there is a scope of meaning, we need to be cautious that we remain inside that scope.

Again, within a passage's specific meaning, there are a limited number of applications that can emerge. When Paul wrote "Put on the new man" (Ephesians 4:24) he was not even remotely instructing a woman to leave her husband and run off with another man (though this indeed was how one woman reportedly applied this passage).[33] We can't just make the text apply in any way we want to, even if it seems to suit our circumstances. The application we draw must fit within the scope of meaning of the passage, or the truth we set out to discover from God's Word becomes neutralized. It becomes about us and what we want and not His desire for us.

Application of the Bible's meaning is practical obedience to God. We are doing what our Lord desires. That's why getting the right meaning is so important. If we get the wrong meaning, we certainly wind up with the wrong application. And even while our intentions may be good, and He knows our heart, we could be heading down a road that ultimately leads us away from Him. But with proper understanding that "all Scripture is God-breathed and is useful for teaching, rebuking, correcting and training in righteousness, so that the servant of God may be

---

33 Koukl, Greg. "Solid Ground Cover Letter." Letter. 1 Sept. 2005. MS. N.p.

thoroughly equipped for every good work," we can discover the personal applications that the Holy Spirit has for us. And this will bring us closer to our God.

Conclusion

While some of this might seem a bit academic, the process of discovering the right meaning is an important one that is worth our efforts. Just as accurate understanding of God's Word brings us closer in line with His desire for our lives, inaccurate understanding takes us away. Moreover, the Bible itself tells us that God's Word is a treasure which should be guarded.

Being diligent to properly understand Scripture shouldn't dull our reading of the Bible at all. Rather, it should actually help the Bible come alive even more for us, as we discover the meaning which the Holy Spirit actually intended for all readers through the ages. Once we understand the meaning, the Holy Spirit teaches and guides us thorough personal applications, so that as we learn, we are made more and more like our Lord and Savior, Jesus Christ.

Questions

1. Give an example of something written (other than the Bible or the examples listed in this chapter) that doesn't matter if you know the author's intended meaning. Also, give an example of something where knowing the author's intention does matter.

2. When you go to the Bible, do you primarily look to get some application for yourself or to try to discover what truth God is teaching us through His word, then apply it? Has this chapter caused you to rethink your approach?

3. Can non-believers interpret and get the correct meaning of passages in the Bible?

4. Can you think of any Bible passages that this chapter has caused you to reconsider the way you understand the passage?

5. Discuss the temptation of Christ (Matthew 4:1-11 and Luke 4:1-12). How did Satan misuse Scripture? How did Jesus respond?

6. Describe the difference between descriptive and prescriptive. How does this affect meaning and application?

7. Romans 14:21 says "Don't cause your brother to stumble." If a person was in the midst of a decision to go into either concrete work or framing and came across this verse, would a proper application be deciding to go into concrete work because they could fix areas where people might stumble? What might be an example of an application of this passage?

Chapter 3

Context. Context. Context.

Take a few moments to think of your favorite passage of Scripture. Really. Stop now and take the time to think about it.

Ok, welcome back. Now answer these two questions we discussed in the last chapter. What does the passage mean? How do you apply it?

Next, imagine the human author of that passage is sitting right there next to you. Describe for them what you understand the passage to be saying. How do they react? Do they say: "That's exactly what I meant." Or is there a strange look on their face while they ask, "How did you get that from what I wrote?" Perhaps you're unsure how they would respond?

After reading the first part of this book, some of us may be beginning to wonder if we've been interpreting Scripture properly. We may be having second thoughts about our Bible study methods. So, it's time now to learn our first tool in interpretation. In this chapter, we'll see how significant knowing the context is to discovering the meaning of any verse. The knowledge of context alone will help us get the basic meaning of almost any passage we're looking at. That's how important it is.

Ultimately, when we finish with this discussion, we'll have a much greater confidence in our own ability to discern the correct meaning from a passage of Scripture. And when we visit with the human authors in Heaven, they'll say, "Exactly what I meant! Praise our Lord!"

Truth in Advertising?

Have you ever felt like you were fooled by an ad for a movie? You see a preview which gets you all excited for a new release. The special effects look incredible. The plot looks captivating. As you become more and more intrigued, quotes from movie reviewers are flying across the screen. Words like "sensational" and "fantastic" get you even more eager to see the film. But then you walk out of the theater thinking you just wasted twelve bucks. How does that happen?

Part of the promotion of the 2009 movie *Love Happens* starring Jennifer Aniston included an advertisement that quoted Roger Moore of the Orlando Sentinel saying "Jennifer Aniston at her most engaging." If you thought that was an endorsement for the film, which you most likely would without context, you'd be quite mistaken. The actual quote from Moore's review says "*Love Happens* is a comedy in mourning, a romance so sad that even Jennifer Aniston at her most engaging can't save it."[1] That doesn't sound like an endorsement for the movie! The use of those words by themselves in an ad is just plain

[1] He adds, "Whatever thin potential Love Happens had is utterly botched…Love Happens doesn't bring tears and what's worse, doesn't create sparks." Moore, Roger. "Movie Review: Love Happens -- 2 out of 5 Stars." Tribune Newspaper, 18 Sept. 2009. Web. 19 Dec. 2009. <http://www.orlandosentinel.com/entertainment/orl-movie-review-love-happens,0,4497205.story>.

misrepresentative of the reviewer's thoughts.[2] The words are taken completely out of their context.

By misusing the words in the ad, people believe certain things (like the movie is great) and are driven to action (like going to see the movie). If we're the one duped, then we're justifiably upset by it. But even if we don't feel like we were fooled by the ad, we should be just as upset because the action itself is wrong. And we might be the one duped in the future!

Now we're just talking about movie reviews and wasting twelve bucks on a movie won't cause anyone significant personal harm, but this illustrates that taking something out of its context can grossly mislead people. It can cause them to have false beliefs, or take action on something when they otherwise wouldn't. The practice itself is unjust, if not immoral. If we carry on this practice to things that are more significant, the potential for harm increases. For example, this practice has been noted to go on in the field of alternative medicine.[3] This could lead to serious health issues for its victims. No one would want to take an herbal remedy that was reported in a study to "remove headaches 99.9% of the time" if the actual context added "but results in mortality of 2% of patients."[4]

---

2 There's a webzine "Gelf Magazine" that offers reviews under the title "The Blurbs" that has many of these out of context examples. "Gelf Magazine." *Gelf Magazine*. N.p., n.d. Web. 19 Dec. 2009. <http://www.gelfmagazine.com/>.

3 Robbins, Martin. "Homeopathic Association Misrepresented Evidence to MPs." *The Guardian*. Guardian News and Media Limited, 4 Feb. 2010. Web. 30 Apr. 2013. <http://www.theguardian.com/science/blog/2010/feb/04/homeopathic-association-evidence-commons-committee>. (By the way, I'm not suggesting that all alternative medicine is bad, only that this type of out of context quoting frequently occurs with manufacturers of herbs and homeopathic remedies. *Caveat emptor.*)

4 An actual example is the herbal supplement birthwort which is still sold in many parts of the world for weight loss, pain remedy and more, despite being strongly linked to cancer and kidney failure. (Vergano, Dan. "Herbal 'remedy' May Trigger Widespread Kidney Failure." *USA Today*. Gannett Co. Inc., 16 Apr. 2012. Web. 30 Apr. 2013.

When we consider the Word of God, what the Bible says is much more important than whether or not we see a movie, or even what medicine we choose. *We are talking about our soul!*

While little mistakes certainly won't impact our eternal destination, larger ones could have ramifications not only for us, but others we teach. New religions have been founded from people taking the Word of God out of context! Do you see how there could potentially be significant harm done if a verse is taken to mean something different, perhaps even opposite, of what it actually means?

Context. Context. Context.

All of us have probably used the phrase "You're taking it out of context" at some point in an argument or discussion. What do we mean by it? What is context? Simply, it's the set of conditions surrounding a particular event. It's what's going on at the time. It includes the setting, the background and the circumstances surrounding the situation. It's the who, what, where, when, why and how. And it is incredibly significant for us to know the context in order to determine the accurate meaning.

One of my professors used to say that we've all heard of the three most important things in determining the success of a restaurant: Location. Location. Location. Likewise, in Biblical interpretation, he would say it was: Context. Context. Context. He even made the whole class shout it out over and over to make sure we didn't forget it, and I haven't.[5]

<http://usatoday30.usatoday.com/tech/science/columnist/vergano/story/2012-04-07/do-herbal-remedies-work/54102616/1> and Hvistendahl, Mara. "Common Herbal Supplement Linked to Cancer." *Science AAAS*. N.p., 8 Aug. 2013. Web. 17 Aug. 2013. <http://news.sciencemag.org/health/2013/08/common-herbal-supplement-linked-cancer>.)

[5] Biola University, Spring 2003, Hermeneutics with Professor Ben Shin

The Bible and Context

> A man was searching the Bible for guidance. Not knowing where to look, he decided to simply open the Bible randomly and point his finger to a passage. Wherever his finger would land, he would take it as God instructing him. So he opened his Bible and the first passage he hit was Matthew 27:5 "So Judas threw the money into the temple and left. Then he went away and hanged himself." Not knowing what to make of it, the man tried again, this time landing on Luke 10:37b "Jesus told him, 'Go and do likewise.'" Now completely bewildered, he tried a third time and landed on John 13:27b. "So Jesus told him, 'What you are about to do, do quickly.'"[6] (At this point, hopefully the man decided to get a book on proper Bible interpretation.)

How important is context to the Word of God? Do Bible verses need to be framed in their context, or can we use any set of consecutive words to mean what we desire? As we concluded in the last chapter, passages do not contain multiple meanings; they contain one meaning inspired by the Holy Spirit. One of the most important items that will help us discover the accurate meaning is knowing the context.

---

[6] I've heard this parable many times over the years, but I don't know its original source. Klein, Bloomberg & Hubbard, *Introduction to Biblical Interpretation*, mentions this same sequence of verses on page 160.

Let's say your teenager tells you the following on a school night:

> Mom/Dad, you know I'm trying to be a good Christian, and I never get drunk. But did you know the Bible not only says we shouldn't get drunk, but in fact, it says we shouldn't even sleep! 1 Thessalonians 5:6 says, "So then let us not sleep, as others do, but let us keep awake and be sober." (ESV) So, Jake and I are going to break out the Xbox and pull an all-nighter in the name of Jesus!

Obviously the Bible isn't talking about staying up all night. And to go without sleep on a long-term basis is physically impossible. Intuitively we know our teenage son is not interpreting the Bible correctly, so we send him to bed. However, without knowing the context, what interpretation could we possibly arrive at? What is the meaning of the verse? How do we not sleep the way others do? Are the others non-believers? Was our son partly right and the verse is suggesting we should sleep less? Maybe it means that we shouldn't sleep as others do, so that we are awake more and have more time to share the Gospel? Or should we go to bars at night where drunks are and witness to them there, but make sure not to get drunk with them. That makes some sense. Or maybe our teenager has it backwards. Maybe it means that we should rise early in the morning. That's how the sleep is different. The reason the text adds that we should be sober is because most people back then who stayed up at night were drunk, and then they slept late in the morning. So maybe the passage means that we should have sleep patterns that reflect healthier living?

All of these possible interpretations seem like they would have good outcomes. In the first, if we witness more, then more people come to Christ. In another, it could mean a healthier lifestyle for us, like the old adage "early to bed, early to rise, makes a man healthy, wealthy and wise." So are they wrong?

We tell our teenager that he can't stay up because he's taking the passage out of context. But then if we turn around and adopt one of these interpretations, aren't we doing the exact same thing!? Just because the outcome might be consistent with other parts of Scripture, it doesn't mean that we can abuse the text the same way our teenager was attempting to do.[7] If the author didn't intend to communicate those messages in that passage, we should not consider them. Furthermore, by going down this road, we are missing the actual meaning and a teaching which we should learn and apply.

How can we know these are not possible interpretations of this passage? Simple. Just by reading the immediate context. If we read the whole paragraph around it (5:1-5:11), we would see that sleep is kind of a metaphor for being in darkness and not following God. The actual point of the passage is that we are children of the light who have salvation in Christ, and we should act as such, especially in anticipation of Christ's return. That's a

---

[7] I've sometimes encountered people who still push at this point. They continue to argue that the meaning is ok since they have tested it through the overall "filter" of Scripture. They look at other parts of the Bible and see that their interpretation is not inconsistent; therefore the implication is that their interpretation is ok. The problem with this objection is that it's ignoring the foundational problem. If you say that it's ok to interpret a passage to mean something as long as it's consistent with the "rest of Scripture," what are you measuring the "rest of Scripture" against? If you are consistent with your principle, then you can just make those other passages mean what you want *them* to mean to match up what you're trying to do with the passage in question. You can't ever argue that you land on a stopping point. Why there? Why that point? Either all passages of Scripture have a meaning in their own context, or none do! This is different than using another passage of Scripture to help *clarify* a passage you are looking at. That is actually a very valuable interpretive tool that we will look at in a future chapter.

very different message than stay up and share the Gospel more or have a healthier lifestyle.

We can't pick Bible verses out and use them how we want, just because they appear to fit what we're trying to teach or accomplish. Even if the application we draw out is good, the action is wrong. It doesn't please God if we use His Word to promote what's right, if the way we are using His words is misrepresentative of how He intended them. For example, if we put up a Bible verse on our church marquee designed to scare people into going to church, but the author meant something totally different by it, we would be being deceptive.[8] There is so much truth in Scripture, why would we need to do this anyway?

When we take something out of context from God's Word, we become like the movie advertisers and rob the words of their original meaning. Any significance we apply to them at that point is purely our own subjective viewpoint and devoid of any majestic authority. Context matters.

Literary Context

There are three basic kinds of context. They are: historical context, the type or style of writing and the surrounding literary context.[9] We will focus on literary context here, then discuss the others in future chapters.[10]

---

[8] If we're doing it to be humorous, that's different. Joking that "with God all things are possible" (Matt. 19:26), even a win by the home team, is not the same thing as fraudulently using the Word to scare people into the pews.

[9] Some other authors include the type of writing in the literary context. While it is "literary" in the sense that it is part of the literature, I've chosen to separate it out because of its significance. When I refer to "literary context," I mean the immediate and larger context of the story, the book and the whole Bible.

[10] You might also hear the term "levels" of context. That's not talking about the different kinds. When we say the different "levels" of context, what we're really talking about is how large of a picture we're looking at of the surrounding text. Is it just the paragraph, or the whole book?

Literary context should be looked at like a funnel. We can begin large and narrow down until we arrive at the precise passage we're looking at. In this method, we begin with the broadest context of a passage, which is the entire Bible. As we zoom in we look to find relevant information from the same testament, then the same author, then the same book, then the passages immediately around our passage, and finally arrive at the passage we are studying. Sometimes we may go in the opposite direction; we start with the passage and work our way up. Still, the idea is that we have the contextual funnel that pours out the correct meaning of our passage.

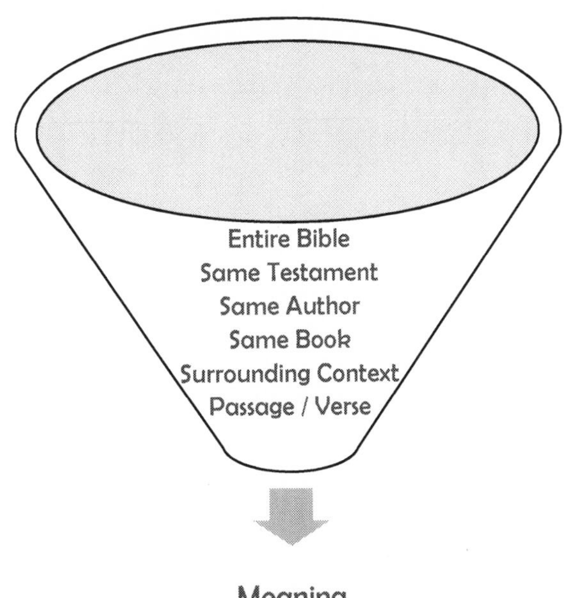

Actually practicing this can be especially challenging because our natural tendency is to quickly focus on a sentence and infer its meaning or context based on the few words we've read. We like sound bites. From television ads to texting, quick sound bites have become a key mode of communication. Our news is Twitter and our social life is a Facebook status update. Moreover, in Sunday school as children, we're taught to memorize individual verses without any surrounding context. While this exercise helps us remember the Word of God, it can cause the verses to become isolated in our minds.[11] Even worse, we sometimes put our own experiences and our own context around those verses. This can lead to erroneous and potentially harmful interpretations of God's message.

What I'm about to say may shock some people, but in the long run it will significantly help your Bible interpretation. Ok. Here goes: *Ignore the reference numbers*! (Ex. Book name 10:5) Yes, except for using them as a tool to find or identify a passage, completely and utterly ignore Bible references! Why? Did you know the original audience didn't have them? In fact, it wasn't until the 1500s that our current chapter and verse notations were fully incorporated.[12] And they have brought with them many potential problems. Sometimes reference numbers show up right in the middle of a thought, causing us to erroneously break it apart. Sometimes they even split sentences. So while reference numbers are helpful to us when we want to look something up (hence, their name), they should never be a part of our interpretative process. They only encourage us to isolate words that weren't necessarily meant to be isolated.[13]

---

[11] I'm certainly not suggesting that we abandon this practice. In fact, I encourage it with my children. I'm only pointing to this practice as a contributing factor to our poor interpretive practices as adults.

[12] The division of the Old Testament verses was complete in about AD 900, though the chapter divisions were not added until centuries later. The New Testament divisions came in the 1500s. (see Klein, Blomberg and Hubbard, *Introduction to Biblical Interpretation*, 159.)

[13] Proverbs may be an exception, but even then often we gain important insight when looking at the collection of Proverbs around any single Proverb, or even the whole chapter.

At the very minimum we should be looking at the pericope. "The what," you ask? (And despite what my word processor thinks, I didn't just misspell periscope.) Pericope (pronounced pe·ric·o·pe) is just a fancy word that refers to a selection of verses that make up the idea or unit of thought. But it's important to know when it comes to Bible study because it's what we should always consider when we are interpreting any one particular passage of Scripture. It gives us the most immediate context. Often just looking at the pericope will help us tremendously. For example, imagine you overheard the following sentence isolated from a conversation: "That surfer is sick." What does it mean? Look at these two short pericopes and see how it is totally different:

> Dude, that was the coolest ride I've ever seen. That surfer is sick. He did a full 360.

> Someone call a doctor. That surfer is sick. He just passed out on the beach.

The same is true when we look at Bible verses. We need to be careful not to isolate words by themselves so that we don't mistakenly use them to mean something they don't mean in their context. Looking at the pericope will many times help us avoid that mistake. Observing the passages surrounding the one in question can give us much of the information that we need. It will frequently help us get the basic meaning. The surrounding passages can tell us the setting (see Luke 19:45 for help interpreting 19:46). They can tell us the audience (see Luke 15:1-3 for help interpreting the parables that follow). They can tell us who the passage is directed to (see Jeremiah 10:1 for help interpreting the following verses). Sometimes when we look at the entire pericope, we even see that the passage is interpreted for us (as in the case of many of Jesus' parables or see Isaiah 5:7 interpreting 5:1-6).

Beyond the pericope, we can also gain information by looking at the larger portions of the book. Sometimes the audience is found several pages back, but nevertheless that information is essential to discovering the right meaning. Stepping even farther out, knowledge of the entire book can help us as well. What are the author's main themes?[14] What's the setting of the book? Is there a particular audience in mind? All of these things can help us to discover the meaning an author intended in a particular passage.

Besides discovering the right meaning, there is another huge benefit to studying this way. The more you read through a book or pericope, the more you will see how it all fits together rather than being an isolated collection of phrases. As you gain a greater understanding of individual passages, you in turn will gain a greater understanding of the author's themes and writing style, which will help you better understand other passages,

---

[14] The theme of a book can be a useful interpretive tool. However, with some books the theme can be a bit ambiguous, and authors may have more than one theme. Learning the theme is something that requires study itself. So what are some ways we can discover theme? (1) Sometimes the author makes a general statement in the beginning of the book. Revelation 1:19 says "Therefore write the things which you have seen, and the things which are, and the things which will take place after these things." (2) Theme can also be discovered by repetition of an idea as in the case of Titus where Christians are repeatedly instructed to maintain integrity and do good works. (3) Occasionally the theme is blatantly clear. For example, Hebrews 8:1 says "Now the main point in what has been said is this: we have such a high priest, who has taken His seat at the right hand of the throne of the Majesty in the heavens" (4) Literary clues or devices can also help us to determining the theme. One example is bracketing or *Inclusio*, a literary device where the text is framed within an idea. This occurs in Psalm 118 which begins with "Give thanks to the LORD, for he is good; his love endures forever." The Psalm ends with the same exact words in verse 29. The author's focus of the entire Psalm is centered on these words.

which helps you better understand the writing style, which... You get the picture. So either start with the larger context and work your way down, or start with your passage and work your way up. The important point is to remember that context plays a significant role in the interpretative process. Knowing it will greatly improve your understanding of the meaning of a particular passage.

Tool #1: Literary Context

As I noted in the introduction, we'll be reviewing "sacred cows." These are verses which are commonly misinterpreted. These examples will help drive our five tools home and make the practice stick better in our memories. Now that we have a basic understanding of the importance of context, let's look at our first "sacred cow" to see the significance of context in action.

Sacred Cow – John 8:32

"You shall know the truth, and the truth shall make you free" (NKJV)

Have you noticed that even as the Ten Commandments are being removed from government and other buildings, that this phrase uttered by Jesus still seems to pop up all over, and never receives the criticism that other Bible quotes often get? "You will know the truth, and the truth shall set you free." Jesus told this to a group of His followers. Today several prominent universities feature this quote on their campus, including: the University of Texas, Miami University (Ohio), the University of Virginia, and Johns Hopkins. This piece of wisdom even gains acceptance from one of the most anti-religious arenas, a public high school in Berkeley, California where it is prominently displayed on campus.[15] A quick search of the internet reveals some of the ways people use the quote: a lawyer has it for his website heading; it's the title of a blog about a murder trial; it's the headline of a news story about the 2008 Chinese gymnastics team; and it's a banner for a webpage about homosexuals "coming out."

There are typically two common misinterpretations that people have of what Jesus was saying here. One is more in line with how the schools see it, with the emphasis on knowledge. The thinking is that the knowledge of the truth allows you to have more freedom because your mind is released from its limited capacity you had before you knew. The idea is that the more you learn and know, the more freedom you will have. The other misinterpretation usually drops the first half of the verse and just goes with "the truth shall set you free." This is the way the webpages are using it. The idea is something like: Coming clean will make you feel relieved (free) because you won't have to hide (the truth) anymore. While there is some wisdom in both of these concepts,[16] are either really what Jesus meant on this occasion? Is "filling their heads with more knowledge" what Jesus is instructing his followers to do? Is "setting our conscience free so we can feel good" the proper application of this passage?

---

[15] Berkeley High School at the corner of Martin Luther King Jr. Way and Allston Way

[16] Again, I say "some wisdom." Telling the truth about something may set our conscience free because we're no longer emotionally struggling with an issue. However, telling the truth doesn't always set you free. For example, truth would not set the spies free when Rahab lied to protect them. The truth would have killed them. Rahab would have been condemned along with the rest of Jericho. And as far as the other way of looking at it, more knowledge doesn't always set us free. It's easy to think of a time in our lives when we learned something we wish we hadn't. Contrary to being free, we are sometimes then captive to the new information.

As we noted above, we should look at the larger context to help us understand the meaning of the specific passage. So for a passage from the Gospel of John, we often will start with thinking about the larger context of the Bible, then the New Testament, then looking at other writings by John and finally considering any themes or related issues in other parts of this Gospel. However, for this chapter, let's just look at the immediate context (the pericope) so we can see the significance of only having that information for helping us interpret our verse. John 8:31-36 (NKJV) says:

> 31 Then Jesus said to those Jews who believed Him, "If you abide in My word, you are My disciples indeed. 32 And you shall know the truth, and the truth shall make you free." 33 They answered Him, "We are Abraham's descendants, and have never been in bondage to anyone. How can You say, 'You will be made free'?" 34 Jesus answered them, "Most assuredly, I say to you, whoever commits sin is a slave of sin. 35 And a slave does not abide in the house forever, but a son abides forever. 36 Therefore if the Son makes you free, you shall be free indeed. (Yes, I left the verse numbers there so we can reference them.)

The first thing that should jump out at us is that Jesus doesn't say "you will *tell* the truth" and the truth will make you free. He says you will "know" the truth. So, it's knowledge of a truth that sets us free, not us telling the truth. That rules out the second common misinterpretation completely. Another thing we can see is that the emphasis here is not as much about knowledge as it is about freedom. The first part of the passage builds up to the culmination in verse 36. "*Therefore* if the Son makes you free, you shall be free indeed."

We are set free by the Son. Free from what? The context tells us. We see that Jesus sets us free from being a slave to sin (verse 34). How? We are set free because we have a knowledge of a certain truth (verse 32). Knowledge of what truth? Well again, let's look at the context. Jesus tells the disciples what truth He is talking about. He says "if you continue in my word, then you are truly disciples of mine; and you will know the truth" (verse 31). It's all found in the periscope. First, notice that the promise is conditional. *If* we do something, *then* we get the result. It's simple. *If* we follow in His teaching, *then* we will experience the result. But it's not just "intellectual truth" or mere "mental assent" that Jesus is talking about. It's an experiential truth. It is the truth that when we abide in His instruction and allow it to transform us, He will disciple us. It comes with the freedom of knowing that our sins are cast on the cross. It's a freedom God wants us to experience in our lives through trusting in Him. And *that* is a truth worth plastering on our walls.

We can see how looking at the literary context around our passage allows us to arrive at the meaning God intended in the passage. This simple practice will greatly aid our Bible studies and help draw us into that experiential truth we long for. Next, let's look at a clever play on words to help us remember this insight.

Two Great Pieces of Wisdom for Bible Interpretation

> "If there was one bit of wisdom, one rule of thumb, one single skill I could impart, one useful tip I could leave that would serve you well the rest of your life, what would it be? What is the single most important practical

> skill I've ever learned as a Christian? Here it is: *Never read a Bible verse.* That's right, never read a Bible *verse.* Instead, always read a paragraph at least." – Greg Koukl[17]

This really is one of the greatest pieces of wisdom I've ever learned about Bible interpretation. It has helped me with numerous passages. If we follow this advice, it assures us that we will at least look at the immediate context. Even if we're not familiar with the whole Bible, or the particular author, or even much of that particular book of the Bible, just reading the paragraph around the passage we're trying to interpret will help tremendously as we just saw in our example of John 8:32.

Koukl also offers another excellent tool that I have employed many times and consider it the other great piece of wisdom for Bible interpretation. He calls it the "paraphrase principle."[18] It's very easy to use and will almost always rule out poor interpretations. "Here's how it works. Just replace the text in question with your paraphrase [your summation of the verse in your own words] and see if the passage still makes sense in light of the larger context."[19]

Let's try using it on the John 8:32 passage. First, try reading the whole paragraph (John 8:31-36), but replace 8:32 with the following misunderstanding, "When you're trapped in a lie, telling the truth sets you free." It just doesn't fit. Now try the other option, "More knowledge about the world will set you free." Neither of them work. It's obvious when you put one of those summaries in the context of what Jesus is saying that both

---

17 Greg Koukl "Never Read a Bible Verse" accessed at http://www.str.org/site/News2?page=NewsArticle&id=5466 on 4/2/10.

18 Koukl, Gregory. *Never Read a Bible Verse "The Most Important Thing I Could Ever Teach You"* N.p.: Stand to Reason, n.d., 3. Print.

19 Ibid, 3.

of them are misuses of Jesus' words. This simple paraphrase test will often help you rule out erroneous ideas.

Conclusion

"Context. Context. Context."

That's all there is to say (or shout if you wish).

Questions

1. What role does the context of a verse or phrase play in understanding the correct meaning?

2. Can you think of an example of a passage that you've heard pulled out of its context?

3. What potential harm might happen if you convinced a friend to come to church by using a Bible verse completely out of context? What might your seeking friend think when he/she discovers the passage was like a movie preview?

4. Look at John 15:7. What does Jesus mean by this statement?

5. John 12:32 is sometimes quoted during worship, saying that we should "lift God up" and exalt Him in our worship, and as a result He will draw us near. Examine the context. Do you think this is an accurate application of John 12:32? What do you think this passage means?

6. Try using the paraphrase principle on some of your favorite passages of Scripture. Does your paraphrase work? Are you understanding the passages correctly?

Chapter 4

In Style

Let's say we hear the phrase "Phil choked." What does it mean? How do we know? As we noted in the last chapter, if we had the complete context we'd get a much better idea. However, there's another piece of information that would give us a strong sense of what the phrase meant, even before knowing the context. That information is the type, or genre, of writing.

Thanks to the technology of iPods and MP3 players, most people are now familiar with the word "genre." It's how we classify our different categories of music: rock, country, alternative, classical, etc. And as with music, literature also has many classifications. When we walk into a bookstore, there are numerous sections separating the different types, or genres, of literature. We can see the signs all around the store. It should be obvious that we don't go to the horror section to pick up a romance novel, even though some guys might think so. Different genres have different purposes and, are often for different audiences.

So, what does the phrase "Phil choked" mean? If we were told it came from a mystery novel, we'd probably think that a person named Phil choked and died. However, if we were told it came from an ESPN news report, we might think that, once again, Phil Mickelson blew a lead on the golf course. Knowing the genre from which a phrase comes can help us interpret what we're reading, and it's not any different with God's Word.

Composed of 66 books, with dozens of different authors, writing for different purposes and to different audiences, one would expect the Bible to be filled with many different styles. From poetry to history, from parables to law, the different genres found throughout the Bible are vast. While covering the complete list of genres in the Bible is far beyond the scope of this book, we can look at a couple of Biblical genres to illustrate why knowing what the genre is matters when it comes to interpretation.

The Genre of Old Testament Law

Do you follow the Old Testament laws? All of them? Do you steer clear of the worship of idols? Are you sure not to steal and not to attempt to seek revenge? Most of us try, and are fairly successful at avoiding those actions. But at your last haircut, did you make sure that the stylist didn't trim your sideburns? (Lev. 19:27) And did you remember to put on your blue tassels this morning? (Num. 15:38) If not, then how do you decide which laws of the Old Testament you should follow and which, if any, don't apply to you?

Certainly, it would seem wise to honor our parents as directed in the Ten Commandments. On the other hand, should we have our children stoned to death if they are stubborn and rebellious? (Deut. 21:18-21) Both of these are commandments in the Old Testament. How can we be consistent and follow one and not the other? Can we just say, I like this one, but that's a little harsh, so that one doesn't apply? That's more like treating the text the way many of us treat traffic rules than it is treating it as the Word of God. So just how do we know?

If we asked most Christians why murder is wrong or why we should obey our parents, the majority would probably point to Old Testament laws. Yet, those same Christians likely have clothes in their closet that disregards Leviticus 19:19, which commands that garments made of two different kinds of material should not be worn. That's right. There's an Old Testament law which says "you shall not sow your field with two kinds of seed, nor wear a garment upon you of two kinds of material mixed together" (NASB). If we were required to follow this, I know I've got a few of my favorite shirts that would be headed for the local thrift shop, not to mention the problem I'd have with deciding what to do about my Bermuda grass lawn which I just over seeded with Rye for the winter. And what about the laws that prohibit eating pork? How many of us might get up on a Sunday morning and have a conversation like this:

> "Dad I don't want to go to church today."
>
> "But son, God wants us to go. And the Bible says we need to honor the Sabbath." [1]

Then later, we get home and for dinner enjoy a nice rack of barbequed baby back ribs? Either we're making a huge mistake before God by disregarding His commands or there has to be some way to make a distinction.

---

1 Few realize that this is actually a different day too. For Jews it was Saturday.

Which Laws Are For Today?

A common approach to traditionally answer this question was to begin by dividing the law into three categories: ceremonial, civil and moral. This is followed by the suggestion that whichever of the three the law falls in to, tells us how to apply it today. So, for example, "Do not murder" (Ex. 20:13), a moral law, would be considered to be a timeless truth and binding today, while wearing blue tassels on our clothing would be considered ceremonial, and like civil laws, were only for the Jewish nation at that time.

There are a number of problems with this approach. For one, the Bible doesn't divide the laws this way. And if the Bible doesn't make this distinction, even for New Testament believers, then we should at least be careful before labeling them as such. A related and perhaps more significant problem is that placing laws in these categories is sometimes arbitrary. Who decides what group to place each law in? Sure, some laws, like those above, appear to easily fall into a category, but some are much more difficult. For example, is keeping the Sabbath a moral law or ceremonial law? It's found among the Ten Commandments, the rest of which certainly seem to be moral laws. So does that mean we shouldn't be doing any work on Sunday? (Lev. 23:3) We might have a real dilemma if we had to stop and pump gas on the way to church. Alternatively, was observing the Sabbath a ceremonial law just for Israel? Was it just part of their system of religious rituals, with no bearing at all for us today? We had better get it right because the Bible says the penalty for not keeping the Sabbath is death! (Ex. 31:14-15, Num. 15:32-36)

Classifying the Sabbath as a moral law seems to put too much emphasis on doing works to earn our salvation. Yet, if we classify obedience to the Sabbath as purely ceremonial for Israel, then we miss important lessons about setting things apart for God, remembering He is the Creator, and the reminder the Sabbath can serve to us of the rest we enter with Him (Heb. 4:1-11). That's why the traditional way of approaching the law just doesn't work.

Who Is the Law Written to?

Knowing some basic principles of Bible interpretation for the genre of law will give anyone a good start to being able to determine how the Old Testament laws apply today. We just critiqued the traditional way of classifying the law into the three categories of ceremonial, civil and moral. While that system doesn't work, note that that it has at its root two important notions which need to be considered: (1) the Church is not Israel and (2) a distinction in the way the laws apply to the Church versus the way they applied to Israel needs to be made. Part of the interpretive problem is simply that the Old Testament laws were not written to believers today, but we often read select ones that way. We fight for posting the Ten Commandments in government buildings as if they were written for America. Yet, the fact is that these laws were not written to American Christians, or Russian Christians, or Jewish Christians or any Christians for that matter.

If Moses had written a separate book of laws and indicated that they were to be a set of timeless rules for the people of God to follow, that would be different. However, that's not what we have with the Mosaic Law. Instead, we have a group of laws recorded throughout the historical records of a particular nation. Recall our discussion on the differences between descriptive and prescriptive literature. The laws in the Old Testament are part of the descriptive story of Israel and cannot be accurately understood apart from that narrative.[2]

Much of the law comes in large portions throughout the Scriptures, and it is being directed to Israel as part of their ongoing relationship with God. To put it simply, *all of the Old Testament laws* were written to Israel, and for Israel. They are part of a narrative that is the record of the relationship between God and His chosen people.

Before we jump to an extreme and say the Old Testament laws have nothing to offer us, we must realize that God put them in our Holy Scriptures for a purpose. It's not included just so we can have a bigger book to hit people with when we go Bible thumping. The history of Israel is important for us to gain insight from and the laws were part of that history. Without the recording of the laws, the history (and more specifically, a major part of the grand story) would be incomplete and more difficult to understand. The laws give us perspective with which to better appreciate God's plan for Israel and Israel's response to God, as well as the fulfillment of God's plan in Jesus Christ. When we see how these relationships work, we discover more about Him, and our purpose. That is the significance for us.

Application of the Law

In Galatians 3:23-25 Paul says,

> "Before this faith [in Jesus as Savior] came, we were held prisoners by the law, locked up until faith should be revealed. So the law was put in charge to lead us to

---

[2] So much of what is labeled "contradictions" in the Bible by skeptics would be easily dismissed if people just understood the importance of genre.

> Christ that we might be justified by faith. Now that faith has come, we are no longer under the supervision of the law." (NIV)

So based on what Paul says here, do we even need the laws anymore? When looking for application, can we now skip over them? Of course not! In fact, just before Paul made this statement, he indicates that the law is not opposed to the promises of God (Galatians 3:21), that it has a purpose. And remember, Paul also said that "All Scripture is God-breathed and is useful for teaching, rebuking, correcting and training in righteousness" (2 Tim. 3:16). So then, how do we apply the laws today?

Biblical interpretation scholars have offered a possible answer that is sometimes referred to as "principlism." One scholar, who has written on this approach, is J. Daniel Hays. He suggests five steps for interpreting and finding significance from Old Testament law.[3]

1. Identify what the particular law meant to the initial audience
2. Determine the difference between the initial audience and believers today
3. Develop universal principles from the text
4. Correlate the principle with New Testament teaching
5. Apply the modified universal principle today

Here are a couple of examples to help see how this process works.

---

[3] J. Daniel Hays, "Applying the Old Testament Law Today," *Bibliotheca Sacra* 158 (2001): 21-35.

Example 1

Let's start with an easy one. "Thou shalt not steal." (Ex. 20:15)

> *Step 1* – To Israel, the original audience, it simply meant "don't steal".
>
> *Step 2* – Believers today are under the New Covenant and this is a Mosaic law, but this law doesn't appear to be anything that would be related to Israel specifically. It's not like God told the Israelites not to steal because if they did the Canaanites would come kill them just because Canaanites don't like thieves.
>
> *Step 3* – The universal principle is just that we should not take something that doesn't belong to us.
>
> *Step 4* – It is reinforced in the New Testament (Romans 13:9, Ephesians 4:28).
>
> *Step 5* – So, applied today it means just what is says, don't steal.

Example 2

Years ago, while studying the book of Joshua, a friend of mine went through a temporary "crisis of faith." When we hit chapter 5, we saw how the Israelites who had been born during the nation's wandering in the desert were uncircumcised. God told Joshua to have all the people circumcised in order to enter back into the covenant relationship with Him. My uncircumcised friend was briefly freaked out about the possibility of having to go through the procedure as an adult. He was quite relieved at the answer we found after we dove into the question. (With this example, I've included questions in the steps that may make the process easier.)

Step 1 – What did it mean to the initial audience? Circumcision was required in the Mosaic Law (Leviticus 12:2-3). This requirement was based on the covenant God had made with Abraham back in Genesis chapter 17. The Israelites could not enter the Promised Land if they were not faithful to the covenant (Genesis 17:14). This was between Israel and God.

Step 2 – What are the differences between the initial audience and believers today? Believers today are under a new covenant. Jesus came and fulfilled the law (Matthew 5:17) and established a new covenant for us (Luke 22:20).

Step 3 – What is the universal principle? The Israelites were ending their wandering in the desert and now wanting to fulfill their end of the covenant with God. At certain times in our walk with the Lord, we may drift away or become complacent. When we get refocused, if there was something we should have done for God that we have not yet done, we should do it. The principle is to get right with God.

Step 4 – How does the New Testament modify, or qualify, this principle? The New Testament teaches that real circumcision is of the heart (Romans 2:25-29, Galatians 5:2-6, Colossians 2:11-14). It's about an inward transformation (getting right with God) and in the physical sense is not necessary for the believer (Acts 15, 1 Corinthians 7:17-20).

Step 5 – How should Christians today apply this principle? Joshua chapter 5 doesn't mean that we need to physically circumcise ourselves and our children today. Instead, we need to make sure that we have circumcised hearts.[4] We need to get right with God. In that sense, the law applies to us and we are compelled to act.[5]

Tool #2: Know the Genre

Prophecy is another of the more common genres found in the Bible. The label "prophecy" can be confusing, as it can conjure up thoughts of clandestine future plans that God has for the world with multi-headed beasts, fiery hail raining from the sky and strange horsemen bringing calamities to the world. But when discussing Biblical genres, scholars separate that kind of symbolic imagery from general prophecy. In Biblical interpretation, predictions about the end of times and other figurative descriptions about God's mysterious plans are often referred to as apocalyptic prophecy.[6] Occasionally, the Old

---

[4] This is not meant to suggest that this is the only application for modern believers. On the contrary, it could also be shown that to Israel circumcision served as a practice, or ritual, that reminded them of their relationship with God. In a similar way, baptism serves a similar function to the modern believer.

[5] Of course, I'm not advocating works theology, as we are saved by grace alone, but if we desire to be followers of Christ, then we ought to certainly attempt to act in a manner consistent with His moral character (John 15:4) and the principles taught in Scripture.

If you're still feeling like the reading Old Testament law is boring to you, stop right now and take the time to get on the internet and read this blog post. The author offers a wonderful example of how the law can provide application to the modern believer. Kimberley, Tim. "The Mistake of Leviticus." Web log post. *Parchment & Pen Blog.* Credo House Ministries, 25 July 2012. Web. 24 Sept. 2012. <www.reclaimingthemind.org/blog/2012/07/the-mistake-of-leviticus/>. It's fantastic.

[6] Depending on one's view of the end times, different labels and distinctions are used. However, when it comes to interpretive principles to use when approaching

Testament prophets do offer this type of prediction, but it's actually not common. When they do offer predictions about the future, it's usually shorter term and part of a "repent or else" type of warning from God. Instead, prophecy in the Old Testament is mostly the "Thus sayeth the Lord" stuff. It's when God's message is being proclaimed to the people through His chosen spokesperson, a prophet.

Like the Law, the books of the Old Testament prophets were written to Israel. They also have a purpose in the grand story of God's plan. The aim of the Old Testament prophets was to call the people away from their sin and to direct them to live for God. The words they spoke were God's warnings to His chosen people that they should repent or they would endure consequences. As with the law, when we interpret and apply prophecy, we need to keep this in mind. Our second sacred cow comes from a prophecy given by Jeremiah. As we attempt to discover the meaning of this passage, we will incorporate both of the tools we have learned to this point: literary context and genre.

Sacred Cow – Jeremiah 29:11

"For I know the plans I have for you," declares the LORD, "plans to prosper you and not to harm you, plans to give you hope and a future." (NIV)

This passage is often cited, especially in motivational type sermons, as a proof text for God having an individual will where He plans to bless each and every one of us in a special way. The

---

different genres, the book of Revelation is treated differently than other books and prophetic passages.

dialog goes something like this: "God has a special plan for you. He says in Jeremiah 29:11 that he plans to prosper you and to give you hope, to give you a future. God loves you and He wants you to know that you are special."

Wow. This is great news. God has an individual plan. For me! And I'm going to be healthy, and wealthy and all that good stuff. That's it. Close the book. Lesson done for the week. Go home and wait for the success and better times to arrive.

How many of us actually look up anything more than the words on the screen or in the bulletin? How many of us actually look at the whole passage and consider the context? How many of us consider what genre the passage came from? As we noted in the last chapter, when we forget to consider context, not only do we set ourselves up to draw from the text something that isn't there, but we also risk missing the real message of the passage. We could miss what God actually intends for us to learn from the passage. And the same can be true if we ignore the genre.

To Whom It May Concern

Suppose that you went to your mailbox tomorrow and you found a note with the following: "The Porsche is parked in spot 27, with the keys in a small box under the front, right wheel well. Take care of it until I get back next month. Feel free to drive it as much as you like." Sounds great, right? The problem is that the note isn't addressed to you. It's written to your neighbor, Sarah. One of her friends must have dropped it in the wrong box. Now do you go cruising in the Porsche? Tempting, but of course not, or you may find yourself spending the night in a cold cell. Why? Because, the top of the note says "Dear Sarah," and you're not Sarah! So, if you wouldn't do that with a note about a car, even a really hot car, why would you even consider doing it with the Word of God?

Remembering our context lessons from chapter 3, let's have a look at what's going on in the verses around verse 11. The beginning of chapter 29 reads "This is the text of the letter that the prophet Jeremiah sent from Jerusalem to the surviving elders among the exiles and to the priests, the prophets and all the other people Nebuchadnezzar had carried into exile from Jerusalem to Babylon." (NIV) There's our "Dear Sarah." The beginning of this passage tells us who the passage is written to. And if that's not enough, verse 4 reads "This is what the LORD Almighty, the God of Israel, says to all those I carried into exile from Jerusalem to Babylon." (NIV) How much more clear can it get? One study Bible I use even has a heading to the chapter to help aid the reader "Message to the Exiles."

Now look at verse 10, which precedes our verse "This is what the LORD says: 'When seventy years are completed for Babylon, I will come to you and fulfill my gracious promise to bring you back to this place.'" (NIV) This flows right in to verse 11. God is saying, through His prophet, that He has a plan for the exiles. He wants them to know that after 70 years, He will rescue them, and return them to Jerusalem. He has a future planned, for the people addressed in verses 1 and 4, *for the exiles.*

As we noted, the genre of this passage is prophecy. This is a specific message God had for His people at the time the prophet delivered it. It is a particular type of communication He chose to use to send a message to a particular people. The context also clearly shows that this verse is specific to God's people exiled in Babylon at the time. When we fail to understand the genre and to see this verse in its literary context, we are led to the false conclusion that the "you" in verse 11 is singular, and is talking about "me" when it's actually plural, and talking about other people. This dramatically impacts the meaning, and thus the application that we draw from the text.

Is There Significance for Us?

What about God having an individual plan of prosperity for your life? That *may* be the case, but if so, we're going to have to find it taught elsewhere in Scripture, because it's simply not here in this passage.[7] That much should be obvious now. Does that mean that the Old Testament is just an interesting history book filled with stories of a people with no real significance for us today? Is that all there is to it? On the contrary, as we've been discussing, this verse, like much of the Old Testament is full of application for modern Christians. It's just that we have to look at the story, and understand the context and the genre of a passage, in order to find how it applies to us.

As we discovered in chapter 2, we must first find the meaning of a passage before we draw out an application. The meaning in Jeremiah 29:11 is much more apparent after we see that it is prophecy given by God to His chosen people of Israel. Through the prophet Jeremiah, God is delivering a message to the exiles. God wants them to know that He has plans for the nation. He is not abandoning them. God has purposes that go back to the original covenant relationship that He made with Abraham, and He intends to fulfill His plans.

A key for the modern reader to help understand the significance of Old Testament prophecy is to see that, just as God's law was written down by Moses for the people of Israel,

---

[7] In fact, the New Testament frequently teaches the opposite for Christians. Many passages indicate that we are called to suffer. (Romans 8:16-17, John 15:18-20, 1 Peter 2:21, Philippians 1:29-30, Paul as described in Acts 9:15-16)

the Old Testament prophets were delivering God's message to Israel. Thus, as with interpreting the law, we need to look at the big picture and understand what is going on with the relationship between God and the people for us to gain insight into a passage. In the case of Jeremiah 29:11, as is the case for much of the Old Testament, God is actively in a relationship with His chosen people who have sinned against Him and He desires them to turn back to Him.

Jeremiah 29 comes after nearly an entire book of "repent or else" prophecies from Jeremiah. Ultimately Israel does not repent and are carried off to Babylon.[8] Then, in their complete dejection, we see that God gives the exiles a promise. At the end of 70 years, if they search for Him with all their heart, and call upon Him, they will find Him (verses 12 and 13). And, if we turn to the book of Daniel, we see that about 70 years later, this is just what Daniel does. Recognizing that 70 years have passed, he prays to God,

> "O Lord, the great and awesome God, who keeps his covenant of love with all who love him and obey his commands, we have sinned and done wrong. We have been wicked and have rebelled; we have turned away from your commands and laws." (Daniel 9:4-5, NIV)

---

8 Try reading Jeremiah from the beginning. I bet you'll find after just a few chapters or so that you become weary of hearing the same message of repent over and over again. God keeps telling them to return to Him or else. But they keep sinning. It gets rather depressing. I can only imagine how difficult it was for Jeremiah. Now if as readers we are starting to get bummed out from all the hammering down from Jeremiah's prophecies, then think about the people back then. Over and over again. They didn't listen. Now they are in exile. They needed to hear this message of hope from God.

Daniel recognizes what the nation has done and pleads for mercy and restoration. He prays for what God had promised. And guess what? God delivers on His promise from Jeremiah 29:11! The exiles returned home.

Applying the Passage

So what can the modern reader take from this? For one, we can learn that God is forgiving. He desires to be in covenant relationship with His people and to bless them. He loves Israel and wants them to return to that covenant relationship. Several times in the early chapters of Jeremiah God makes this clear.

The first time I listened to Jeremiah in an audio drama,[9] I remember arriving at chapter 29 and having such a sense of relief and thankfulness to God. Listening to the drama, I tried to put myself into the world of the people in the story, to think what they were thinking and to feel what they were feeling. The exiles were finally realizing that they messed up and perhaps feeling like God had abandoned them. I understood not just mentally, but emotionally that they needed to hear this promise.[10] They experienced God's judgment, but now they needed to know He loved them. I was in tears as I heard verse 29:11. God is so full of love that even if we fight and fight, He opens His arms to comfort us when we finally come running to Him.

God desires to be in a loving relationship with His people, but He asks for their obedience to Him. That is a key principle we can learn from Jeremiah 29. We can apply that practice today.

---

[9] The Word of Promise Audio Bible. I highly recommend this dramatized reading from the NKJV from Thomas Nelson.

[10] This goes back to what we discussed about the Holy Spirit's role in helping the believer absorb significance from the text.

Furthermore, we see this principle reinforced by Jesus own words in John 15:1-11. "Abide in me, and I in you...If you keep my commandments, you will abide in my love...[and] your joy may be made full."

There are other lessons which could be learned from the Jeremiah passage, but God having an individual prosperous plan for our life is just not one of them.[11] It's erroneous to teach that message from this verse. I'm not suggesting that if you have a picture hanging by your door with the inscription of Jeremiah 29:11 on it that you need to pack it away in the attic. Instead, when you see it, you should think about where the passage comes from, a prophecy to Israel, and what God was doing with His people at the time. Then, when you have the accurate meaning, consider how the story can be instructive for you today.

Biblical Genres

We've now looked at the law and prophets, but there are many, many more types of literature in the Bible. The following is a list of some of the more common Biblical genres. The list is not comprehensive and is only meant to provide an overview.[12] The key point of this chapter is to show that knowing the type of

---

11 It's also interesting to point out that it is likely that only a remnant of the people who heard the promise of God through Jeremiah's letter actually experienced it. Many of them would have died by the time of the fulfillment. Their experience was to follow the commands laid out in verses 29:5-9. This only further emphasizes that this was a corporate promise for Israel rather than any kind of individual promise.

12 The following are highly recommended for reading more about Biblical genres: Gordon D. Fee and Douglas Stuart, *How to Read the Bible for All Its Worth* Third Edition (Grand Rapids: Zondervan, 2003); Walt Russell, *Playing with Fire: How the Bible Ignites Changes in Your Soul* (Colorado Springs: NavPress, 2000); and W.W. Klein, C.L. Blomberg and R.L. Hubbard, Jr., *Introduction to Biblical Interpretation* (Nashville: W Publishing Group, 1993), 259-374.

writing can give us clues about the author's intent, the primary audience, the purpose, and more, all of which will help us discover the correct meaning of a passage. And out of the accurate meaning we can draw an application for our lives today.

Historical Narrative

Historical narrative includes much of the Old Testament, Acts, and a large portion of the Gospels. This type of literature is just like reading a story, a history novel perhaps, though not so much like a modern history book because the authors of the Bible often had a purpose or theme that drove their writing. Much Biblical narrative is describing what happened to the characters involved, but to a specific audience or with certain ideas in mind. Knowing the audience, as well as the purpose and theme, helps us discover the meaning. The books of Chronicles, for example, are basically a recap of much of the same history found in the books of 2 Samuel and 1 and 2 Kings, but to a later audience (the exiles) and with a more religious focus (especially on the Temple), reminding them about living in a covenant relationship with God.

Narratives can capture us because they are "Real lives, real situations, real challenges [and] real responses. Narrative engages us, and that is exactly the way God would have it. Why? Because He seeks to engage us."[13] God teaches us through the stories of others. Furthermore, stories are memorable. Everyone who does public speaking knows that including stories significantly enhances a presentation as well as the audience's memory of the presentation. For example, you may not remember many of the

---

[13] Mead, Peter. "Narrative Lived." Web log post. *Biblical Preaching.* N.p., 25 Aug. 2012. Web. 24 Sept. 2012. <http://networkedblogs.com/BmqGM>.

details from chapter 1, but I bet you remember the story of my aunt freaking out about my NASB Bible.

Still, we need to be careful not to read historical narratives as "how to manuals." While many of the stories of individuals can provide good examples for us to follow (or in some cases, not to follow), we need to remember that the history books of the Bible simply record what happened, "not necessarily what should have happened or what ought to happen every time."[14] The stories often don't tell us whether the actions of the people are right or wrong. Therefore, we need to be cautious about using the stories as models for behavior today.

When reading historical narrative, we often jump to the stories of the people to look for application exactly for the reasons we just mentioned. They are easy to relate to. But there is one key principle we should always keep in mind when interpreting and applying historical narrative: God is the focus of the grand story. It is not about us. It is not even primarily about Israel. It is about Him. Therefore, when we read though narratives, the primary lessons we should be looking for are what the passages teach us about God's character and His eternal plans for the world. As we look for application, we should be asking how we can contribute to those plans. In what ways can we be used by Him to bring about His purposes?

So, rather than starting with the people in the story, and making some assumptions about their behavior, begin studying narratives by looking for what they teach about God. Make that the focus. Then, secondarily, examine the people and their actions to look for some possible life lessons or principles that can be learned from their behavior.

---

[14] Fee & Stewart, 106

Genealogy

Genealogies are not just a bunch of names that we should jump over (although I wouldn't recommend trying to read them out loud without first consulting a pronunciation key. I've personally made a couple of rather embarrassing mistakes). Lineage was indeed important for Israel, and thus genealogies are often recorded. In the case of Christ, for example, it shows confirmation that Jesus is from the line of David, as promised. So when you come across a genealogy, ask "What's the purpose of this? Why is this included here? What significance did it have to the original audience?"

Poetic Literature

This is the poetry, songs and prayers in the Bible. Poetic literature includes the Psalms and Song of Solomon, as well as expressions of praise such as the Song of Mary (often called the *Magnificat*) found in Luke 1:46-55. It's very different than the genres we've noted so far. It's so much more personal. I'm thankful that God made poetic literature such a large part of the Scriptures. You can't learn everything from just facts. Imagine the Bible without the book of Psalms! For example, what if we only had the story of David and his sin with Bathsheba, and were not able to read his repentant heart in Psalm 51? Biblical poetry lets us see the hearts of people when they bare them before God. It shows us how they felt, and often helps us relate to God in the same way.

To talk about finding the meaning in poetic literature can seem hollow, because it is filled with so much emotion. Nevertheless, we should keep in mind some simple principles. As with all of Scripture, we don't want to pull a passage away from its context and use it apart from the meaning that was originally inspired by the Holy Spirit.

What are some good principles for interpreting Biblical poetry? First, since Biblical poems, songs and prayers were composed as units, they should be interpreted that way. Much like a modern song which has a theme, the authors of poetic literature had specific ideas in mind. Was there something that happened to them that led the author to write it? Is there a particular situation they are talking about? We should try to discover the meaning or purpose before pulling out just a single line from the Psalm.[15] Also remember, just like modern poems, they contain figurative and metaphoric language. We shouldn't feel as if we need to interpret everything in a poem as if it's from a science text book.

Another helpful tool is to know what the Psalm was originally used for. Did people sing it in remembrance of a particular event? The early audiences knew better the purpose of the Psalm and learning how they applied it will help us discover what it means and ways we can experience it today.

Proverbs

Proverbs are often mistaken for being a promise or a guarantee, but they are not. They are simply wise sayings. The wisdom of course comes from God, so they are much more significant than something like "a penny saved is a penny earned," but, like other adages, they are only general truths. For

[15] By the way, just a pet peeve, but when you refer to the book it's Psalms. When you refer to an individual chapter or passage, it's Psalm. Often when I hear someone say "Turn to Psalms 46:10 (or any single verse in the book of Psalms)," I want to respond "that is such a good verses." But I usually try to keep my anal retentiveness to myself.

example, Proverbs 14:23 says "All hard work brings a profit, but mere talk leads only to poverty" (NIV). I've known Christians who have worked extremely hard only to see their businesses fail. I'm sure we all have some examples where a Proverb didn't factually come true. Thus, this Proverb is not a promise that *all* hard work will be rewarded with money. However, the principle – in order to make money, you need to work hard and not just talk about it – is certainly a general truth. Proverbs should be read in this light.[16]

Epistles

Have you ever wanted to read someone else's mail? If you're on Facebook, then you may already have your fill. Unless people have changed their privacy settings, you generally will see posts from one person to another in your news feed. Sometimes when I've read what people wrote, it doesn't make a lot of sense. However, the two of them clearly knew what the conversation was about. If I had some background information and perhaps context, that would help fill in the gaps for me and I would better understand the message. This is kind of what it's like when we read the New Testament epistles because that's pretty much what they are: communications from one individual to another (as in the case of the pastoral epistles) or communications to specific churches. Of course, rather than a quick note, the epistles are letters which are much longer. They contain both specific details to certain people, or people groups,

---

[16] It should be noted though, that there are a few Biblical proverbs which are more than just general truths; they might even be considered simple factual statements because they are Proverbs about God. Proverbs 6:16-19 and 11:1, fit into this category.

and prescriptive moral guidance for all members of God's Kingdom.

It is also helpful to know that New Testament epistles generally follow a pattern. The pattern commonly consists of: (1) a salutation or greeting mentioning both the sender and recipient; (2) thanksgiving and/or prayer; (3) the body of the letter; and (4) a closing. Furthermore, the body of many of Paul's letters are divided into two sections. First, he lays out general principles (and often problems within a specific church). Then, he gives recommended practices of behavior for the Christian. Knowing where you are in the epistle will help in the interpretive process. Additionally, having at least some basic knowledge about the audience the letter was written to and the purpose for the letter will also help you discover what the author is communicating.

Finally, there is one area where epistles stand out from other Biblical genres. Epistles, for the most part, are prescriptive. They offer general instructions to the church of the past as well as the church of the present day. They are insights and directions that we ought to follow.[17] Certainly there are occasions where they contain culturally specific guidelines, and the careful interpreter will spend time discerning when this is the case. But as a general rule, the teachings of the New Testament epistles are timeless.

---

17 Some might be wondering here about why the "Dear Sarah" example above doesn't apply the same way to Paul's letters. The simple answer is that Paul's letters were written to churches, which are all part of the Church. We are part of that same Church today. So while there are certainly some cultural aspects of Paul's letters that we need to consider before applying them to us today, much of what Paul instructs to the churches back then is applicable to us today.

Gospels

The Gospels are the books of Matthew, Mark, Luke and John. They are the four stories primarily of the ministry, crucifixion and resurrection of Jesus. The Gospels have some similarities to a modern biography, but they differ in that they only focus on the last few years of Jesus' life. When we study the Gospels, it is often useful to look at parallel accounts. However, this should remain secondary to examining the passage within each writers own book, so that we can focus on and understand that writer's emphasis in the passage.

As it may have occurred to some of us already, sometimes one genre can be in the middle of another. For example, the Song of Mary noted above occurs within the historical narrative of Luke's Gospel. Thus, the Gospels pose an extra challenge to interpret because they are filled with all different kinds of genres: parable, historical narrative, apocalyptic, etc. Genres within genres.[18] Doing some research about interpretive principles for those genres will greatly benefit us.

Finally, when interpreting the Gospels, we need to be sure we first understand what the passage is telling us about Jesus, and then we can look for an application. Bible scholar Walt Russell explains: "[The Gospels] teach us about who Jesus the Messiah is and give us the opportunity to be discipled by Him as we observe Him and His disciples."[19]

---

[18] Gospels aren't the only place where this occurs though. Intermixing of genres occurs throughout the Bible. It just occurs frequently in the Gospels.

[19] Russell, 204-205, 211.

Conclusion

As we are finding out, Bible interpretation is not always an easy process, but it is a worthwhile process. We have to know something about the genre that our passage comes from before we just take it and apply it. Jeremiah 29:11, for example, can't be taken as a single proclamation of blessing to the modern reader, when God never intended it to be. If we do that, why not just arbitrarily pull out any verse and say it applies to us? We need to be careful not to interpret passages like Jeremiah 29:11 to mean what we want just because we like the way they sound for us. For any verse we study, before we draw conclusions about its teaching and application, we should always consider the genre, and how the genre impacts the passage's meaning.

Questions

1. Give an example of how knowing that a passage comes from a certain book might help with its interpretation and application.

2. Considering Jeremiah 29:11 and the way it is often misinterpreted, do all believers actually prosper (in the sense that the verse is often misused)?

3. Jeremiah 29:13 says "You will seek me and find me when you seek me with all your heart." Review the lessons in this chapter with that verse in mind. What could be an application of this passage for the modern believer? What about when you consider Matthew 7:7? Is there a general Biblical principle about seeking God?

4. What may be the principle behind Leviticus 19:19? "Keep my decrees. Do not mate different kinds of animals. Do not plant your field with two kinds of seed. Do not wear clothing woven of two kinds of material."

5. Read Proverbs 22:6. How does understanding the genre impact the application of this passage?

6. In Acts 1:26, Matthias is selected to replace Judas as the twelfth apostle. Should this be a model for churches today to select elders? Why or why not?

Chapter 5

The Backstory

Several years ago my family rented the film *Pearl Harbor* starring Ben Affleck. We popped the DVD into the player and sat down for a relaxing evening. The movie began with a powerful scene of President Roosevelt speaking to his cabinet just after the bombing of Pearl Harbor. The scenes progressed from there to show the initial retaliation of the US on Japan, and the events that followed. We knew the film was about Pearl Harbor, but everything we were watching occurred *after* the Pearl Harbor attack. About 15 minutes into the movie, we all began looking at each other asking, "Does anybody understand what's going on?" Someone suggested that there was probably going to be some sort of flashback, but we all commented on how difficult it was to follow. Considering the poor reviews we'd heard about the film, none of us yet suspected anything else was amiss.

As the movie continued, we had to pause it a couple times to discuss what we thought was happening. We all had different ideas about why the characters acted certain ways to each other. As we eventually learned, the two main characters were best friends who essentially had a disagreement over a girl. Some of us had surmised this, but one person thought the two men had a long term hate for each other which was being juxtaposed against the story of them learning to fight together. Another one of us thought that maybe the two men were brothers. Ideas were flying, with no real consensus or understanding for that matter. Forty-five minutes later when the credits stared rolling on a three hour movie, it confirmed what we all had begun to suspect: There were two discs and I'd put the wrong one in first. D'oh![1]

The Importance of Background Information

As my family and I watched disc two of *Pearl Harbor*, none of us knew if any of our theories about what was happening were correct because we'd missed the entire background from the first part of the movie. In fact, many of the conclusions we had drawn turned out to be wrong. The point of this should be obvious: without the proper background information, it's easy to misunderstand what's going on right in front of us.

When we look at a verse in the Bible without its historical context in mind, the same thing can happen. Without knowing what occurred before the passage, we miss important information that helps us to discern the proper meaning. We lack the full picture of what's going on. And even worse, just like my family and I did with the movie, we might wind up putting our own incorrect interpretive spin on the events.

The Bible is very much a historical book based on a developing relationship between God and the world. Many times, identifying and understanding the stage of that relationship is essential to our figuring out the correct meaning of the text.

---

[1] In my defense, the only place it says it's disc 2 is in small writing on the center of the disc. Once it's in, the screen says nothing about it being part 2! Ok, I still feel like a dork.

Before we go any further, if you don't already have a grasp of the basic story of the Bible, I'd recommend you make that a priority. And I don't mean reading some 500 word overview. It's important to at least learn the big picture, and to know the main characters. For example, there are several major events that occur just in the book of Genesis, including Creation, the Fall, the Flood and the Abrahamic Covenant. We should know some basic information about those events, as well as their progression and the people involved, including Abraham, Isaac, Jacob and Joseph. Many of these details will be instrumental to our proper understanding of later passages.

There are several places we can go to learn about the big picture of the Bible, including books, audio recordings and video series. Many churches also offer their own Sunday school type courses which teach the basics of the Bible. The ministry Stand To Reason[2] has an excellent resource entitled *The Bible Fast Forward* and is available in both audio and video format. Whatever you use, be sure it's from a reputable source. If you're uncertain, ask your pastor or a church leader for a recommendation.

Background Sources

Knowing the big picture and main characters will greatly aid our Bible study, but sometimes we'll find we need to learn more detailed historical information. In addition, there are other kinds of information that are "behind" Bible passages that can help with our understanding. Knowledge of social structures and behavioral norms, economic conditions, the political environment and even geographical information can all aid in

---

[2] Their website is str.org

the accuracy of our interpretation. But that's still not all of it. It's also useful to know things like who the author is, why he wrote the book, when he wrote the book, and who he wrote it to.[3] It may sound daunting, but familiarity with these topics will help provide depth and richness to our understanding of the Bible's message.

Fortunately, if we want to find the cultural and historical background of a specific Bible passage, there are many places we can go. A selection of recommended sources can be found in Appendix 1.

The Bible

The first place to go is the Bible itself. We'll look more at how we can use the Bible to interpret the Bible in the next chapter, but we should note here that sometimes the history behind a passage can be found in other parts of the Bible. For example, when we study from the letters of Paul, it is helpful to know a bit about Paul's experiences in the churches he is writing to. We can discover some of that information in the book of Acts. We can learn about events that occurred on Paul's trip to Thessalonica in Acts chapter 17, and to Corinth in chapter 18. Reading those accounts in Acts helps give us some basic background information that could be useful when we look to find meaning and application from those letters. Likewise, many

---

[3] "God could have supernaturally written His entire Word down – as He did the Ten Commandments (see Exodus 31:18) – and handed it over, but He chose to use men. We can only assume this comes with purpose: There is something worth knowing about every chosen writer." (Hatmaker, Jen. *A Modern Girl's Guide to Bible Study: A Refreshingly Unique Look at God's Word.* Colorado Springs, CO: NavPress, 2006. 115. Print.) Yes, I admit, I read a book with "A Modern Girl's Guide" in the title. You should have seen me on the plane, sitting next to a triathlete, and trying to hide the cover.

stories in the Old Testament can only be properly understood by knowing what occurred previously.

Study Bibles

Introductions, which are frequently found just prior to each book in a study Bible, usually provide an overview of the historical context and other important elements, such as the author, who it was written to and major themes. These summaries are very helpful to review before reading through a book. They can also provide insights to help us interpret some specific passages. Additionally, many study Bibles contain other supplemental entries with more details on the events or topics throughout the book. So if you don't already have one, pick yourself up a good study Bible. There are several options available, including the New Open Bible and the NIV Study Bible. While they are a bit heavier to carry around, a study Bible is definitely worth the extra weight.

Bible Atlases

Learning Biblical geography is also often useful. The Bible writers regularly provide facts about the setting: where people are, where they are headed, and where the story takes place. But while the Bible stories provide the geographical information, they seldom offer many details about it.[4]

As is the case often with historical background, the Bible writers assumed their readers were familiar with the geography.

---

[4] I'm not saying that they never provide details. In fact, apologists often note that the inclusion of non-relevant details provides evidence for the Bible's authenticity and truthfulness. However, in the cases where the details are not provided, a little extra research can provide valuable information which will make your Bible study much richer.

Today, however, many of us are not. This is where Bible Atlases can be very useful. Many Bible atlases are full of pictures and maps which can provide us a helpful picture of the topography, distances and the relationship of different nations. For example, if we were studying the book of Joshua, Bible atlases can show us what route Israelites traveled, where key battles took place, and how the nation divided the land.

Bible Dictionaries

Bible dictionaries are some of the most useful tools when studying historical and cultural background. These dictionaries aren't like what we think of when we envision a copy of Webster's Dictionary. Instead, Bible dictionaries are more like short encyclopedias. They contain more detailed information about people, places, historical items and other entries which aid our study. Additionally, there are also more comprehensive Bible encyclopedias available if we are looking to really dive into a topic.

Commentaries

General commentaries which were mentioned in chapter 2 also have a wealth of information, including background material on many passages.[5] In addition, there are some commentaries designed to specifically help us with background information. These tools are aptly referred to as "Bible Background Commentaries." These are an excellent resource, and one of my personal favorites for Bible study. Unfortunately, there are

---

[5] As I noted before, I prefer to use general commentaries after I've arrived at a basic idea of the passage, so I'm not led in a direction by the commentator.

currently a limited number of background commentaries available.

Other Sources

There are many other sources available to help us with background information including Old and New Testament Surveys, Bible Handbooks and books on Bible History. A word of caution: be sure to investigate the credibility of your sources.[6] For example, one popular error somehow still endures. In Matthew chapter 19, Jesus says it's easier for a camel to go through the eye of a needle than for a rich man to get into heaven. A common myth is that there was a small "camel's gate" leading into Jerusalem referred to as the "eye of the needle" that camels could squeeze through if they got down on their knees and had their packs removed. Sermons have even been preached suggesting that the image of the camel on its knees meant that Jesus wants us to go to Him on our knees. But as Bible scholars Scott DuVall and Daniel Hays so eloquently put it, "Just because background material makes a great sermon illustration does not mean that it is accurate."[7] The problem is that there is simply no evidence to support this story. No such gate has ever been discovered and furthermore no such practice has been found to

---

[6] As a general rule, cable television is not a good source for accurate information about the history of the Bible. Many of these shows, especially those produced from around the 1990s to the early 2000s, feature members of the Jesus Seminar as their so called "experts." This group denies the Deity of Christ, as well as many other orthodox Christian views. These television shows mislead the viewer by labeling these fellows as "Christian" scholars. Additionally, keep in mind that television shows use sensationalism to get people to watch. They're about revenue more than they are about truth. So while sitting down in front of the tube seems like an easy way to get some Bible background knowledge, be cautious of the information.

[7] Duvall and Hayes, 106.

exist anywhere in the world of that time. The "eye of the needle" is just what we think it is: the eye of a sewing needle.[8]

So the lesson is to thoroughly check your sources. Has their research been through examination by other experts in the field? Where did the author(s) go to school? What degree or degrees do they have? What experience in the field do they have? Do they have a particular viewpoint they are arguing for? These kinds of questions will help you recognize whether your source is dependable.

The Value of a Background Check

Many businesses today do background checks on their job applicants. This costs money, so there must be a payoff for them, right? And there is. Background checks validate or invalidate the information that the person has given them. Companies learn about the potential employee's history and occasionally they dig up some really, let's just say, "interesting" material. (Better clean up those Facebook profiles.) This investigation helps the company get a clearer picture than from just a résumé and a few interviews. The additional information helps the hiring manager make a more informed decision to select the right person for the job. And, just as the background check is worth the company's investment, our time and efforts towards background research will pay off in our Bible reading. In particular, there are three significant ways that background information aids and enriches our study.

---

8 Some scholars have suggested that the word "camel" in the passage may actually be "rope." If you're interested in finding our more about that, then here's an opportunity for you to start using your background resources.

Background Knowledge Helps Us Discover the Meaning of Complex Passages

I recall going through a lesson in a Sunday school class in the 1990s where there was some debate about a passage in Revelation. Not surprising as there's generally a lot of debate about passages in that book. But what was unexpected, was that this passage came from the early part of the book, before it gets into all those bizarre animals and puzzling numbers. The passage in question was Revelation 3:15-16. Speaking of the church in Laodicea Jesus said "I know your deeds, that you are neither cold nor hot. I wish you were either one or the other! So, because you are lukewarm—neither hot nor cold—I am about to spit you out of my mouth." (NIV) Cold, hot, lukewarm, spit (or vomit, as some translations have it); what exactly does Jesus mean with this condemnation? Depending on the background information we have, we could arrive at two very different understandings of this passage.

The interpretation being suggested by the zealous young group leader was that Jesus needs us to be on fire for Him (hot). He desires it so much that Jesus stresses the point by saying that even heathens who are lost (cold) are better off than Christians who are laidback (lukewarm). In other words, Jesus would rather have people be hostile to Him than to be a follower and be lackadaisical about their Christianity. At least those hostile to Him are true to their beliefs. Turn or burn, but don't be taciturn!

But is this really what Jesus is saying to the Laodiceans? Does Jesus really regard His enemies higher than those who love Him? It seems that if this interpretation were correct, then we'd have to say that (1) God wants all men to be saved (which we know from 1 Timothy 2:3b-4), but (2) He'd rather you went to hell if you didn't live your life with zeal for Him. Is that really what Jesus means in this passage?

One of the more elderly and learned believers in the group brought forward another suggestion that was based on historical information which we know about Laodicea. He suggested that the "cold" and "hot" were actually references to Laodicea's water supply. The city had no good water of its own, and therefore received its water via aqueducts from the hot springs of Hierapolis or the cold waters of Colossae. By the time the water reached Laodicea from either source, it had turned lukewarm. When Jesus says to the Laodiceans that they are neither hot nor cold, but rather lukewarm, they would have understood the reference to mean that their works (like their waters) were not exceptional in any way. The church in neighboring Hierapolis was known for their healings and nearby Colossae for a vibrant and refreshing ministry.[9] There was nothing remarkable or noteworthy about the Laodiceans. They were just flat. Therefore as the Zondervan Illustrated Bible Backgrounds Commentary (ZIBBC) describes, "lukewarm" in this passage "does not refer to believers who lack zeal or are half-hearted, but rather to those whose works are barren and ineffective."[10] The additional background information leads us to the correct meaning of the passage.

This is a good time to emphasize another caution with background research. While the early readers were familiar with the cultural and historical background (because many of them lived it), the modern reader only knows what they have studied. Sometimes the information from antiquity has been lost, or

---

[9] Osborne, Grant R. *Revelation.* Grand Rapids, MI: Baker Academic, 2002. 205-06. Print.

[10] Wilson, Mark. "Revelation." *Zondervan Illustrated Bible Backgrounds Commentary.* Ed. Clinton E. Arnold. Vol. 4. Grand Rapids, MI: Zondervan, 2002. 276. Print.

remains undiscovered. Today, we rely on scholarship and research to aid us. Archeologists make new discoveries. Anthropologists learn more about ancient people. Linguists refine our translations. When we learn more, it can correct what we previously misunderstood about Scripture. Recall that one of our key goals is to discover what the original author intended to the original audience. If we learn something new about the author or the audience, it follows that it could change our understanding of the passage.

So what do we need to be cautious of? We need to remember that background information can be outdated. In fact, in the case of Revelation 3:15-16, many of the classic commentaries including those of Matthew Henry and John Gill (both widely available on the internet) suggest the first interpretation. Furthermore, Bible software programs, while being great tools which make Bible study faster and more economical, have actually helped perpetuate some of the incorrect older information. The problem is that so many of the sets, in order to keep their own costs down, include older, non-copywrited books which have outdated historical material.[11] I've had firsthand experience with this. The young, immature Christian with zeal that was mentioned above was in fact, me.

In addition to using outdated information when I taught on this passage, I made another significant error. I allowed my own zeal to influence the way I understood this passage. This leads us right into our second benefit of researching the background information.

---

11 I'm not saying that we shouldn't use classic commentaries. On the contrary, the theological greats of the past often provide us valuable insights. What I am suggesting is that in some cases, if those insights were based on flawed or limited knowledge of the historical information, that we should seriously question the interpretation.

Background Knowledge Helps Us See Around Our Own Preconceptions and Cultural Customs

I once had to dress up in old west gear for my daughter's third grade class. I put on a cowboy hat, a western shirt, and a pair of old pointed toe boots. When I got to the school, many of the kids (especially the boys) were laughing at me and pointing at my boots. They were asking why I was wearing high heels. I vigorously protested. "These aren't high heels. They're boots!" But they just kept on laughing. After talking with them, I discovered that most of them knew they were cowboy boots. They were just laughing because other kids were laughing at me too. Kids love to laugh. But a couple of the boys actually said they had never seen a guy wearing boots like mine (particularly with the pointed toe). They had never seen an old west television show, and since we live in San Diego, about all they ever see guys wearing is running shoes, board shoes or flip-flops. They actually believed I was wearing women's shoes! In those boys' world, a pointed shoe with a heel that rises is a ladies shoe. They brought that knowledge with them to the Boom Town event and interpreted my shoes within their frame of reference.

When we approach the Biblical text, like these boys, we bring our frame of reference with us. Without even realizing it, we could force an interpretation on the text just because of our own worldview. There are many examples of how different cultures see the world differently. Some cultures (like our own) are highly individualistic. Others (like ancient Israel) hold to a more collective view. They see the family as the most important source of identity.[12] Some cultures are shame societies, while

---

[12] Richards, E. Randolph, and Brandon J. O'Brien. *Misreading Scripture with Western Eyes: Removing Cultural Blinders to Better Understand the Bible.* Downers Grove, IL: IVP, 2012. Print.

others are guilt based. Some are scientifically minded, some prefer contemplation and meditation. One of the challenges we face is discovering the accurate meaning without reading something from our own cultural experiences or presuppositions into the text.

A good example where this can happen is in 1 Timothy 2:9-10. Paul wrote, "I also want the women to dress modestly, with decency and propriety, adorning themselves, not with elaborate hairstyles or gold or pearls or expensive clothes, but with good deeds, appropriate for women who profess to worship God." Many of us would read "dress modestly" as a call for the women in the church to not wear revealing or sexually alluring clothing. In America we have a culture that uses images of scantily dressed women to sell goods. We have a problem with internet pornography. We face a battle with our daughters to get them to dress modestly while many of the girls they watch on TV and see in magazines don't. Sexually tempting clothes are everywhere in our culture. No wonder we would automatically interpret Paul's words this way. But is that what he means?

The ZIBBC offers the following entry for 1 Timothy 2:9:

> "It was customary for women in ancient Greek cities to dress up in their very finest for public worship festivals...Even the cult statues of goddesses were adorned in great finery at public festivals...In contrast to the prevailing practice, Paul instructs women (and, by implication, men as well) to focus their attention not on rich wardrobes, but on the inner beauty of Christian character."[13]

---

[13] Baugh, S. M. "1 Timothy." *Zondervan Illustrated Bible Backgrounds Commentary*. Ed. Clinton E. Arnold. Vol. 3. Grand Rapids, MI: Zondervan, 2002. 456. Print.

Paul is not focused on sexually revealing clothing.[14] He's talking about wearing clothes that say to other people "I have money." That's why he adds that women should not adorn themselves with "elaborate hairstyles or gold or pearls or expensive clothes." All of a sudden this verse goes from a passing passage that we think we have become proficient at, i.e. dressing *sexually* modest, to a convicting lesson for us about dressing *economically* modest.[15] Without the background knowledge, we might miss this important message.

Background Knowledge Brings Depth and Richness to Our Bible Study

Knowing the background helps us get so much more out of a passage. In Matthew 11:21-22, Jesus says,

> "Woe to you, Chorazin! Woe to you, Bethsaida! For if the miracles that were performed in you had been performed in Tyre and Sidon, they would have repented long ago in sackcloth and ashes. But I tell you, it will be more bearable for Tyre and Sidon on the day of judgment than for you." (NIV)

The basic meaning of the text is clear. Jesus is warning Chorazin and Bethsaida of judgment. Verse 20 informs the reader that these two towns were the two places where Jesus performed most of his miracles, and yet the people of these towns refused to repent, so Jesus issues them a warning.

---

[14] I'm certainly not suggesting it's ok to dress in sexually revealing clothes. I'm only saying that the teaching is not what Paul has primarily in mind here.

[15] Richards, E. Randolph, and Brandon J. O'Brien. *Misreading Scripture with Western Eyes: Removing Cultural Blinders to Better Understand the Bible.* Downers Grove, IL: IVP, 2012. 42-45. Print.

We could stop our Bible study here if we chose. We might come up with a personal application like "it is wise to repent and follow Jesus" or "miracles teach us to be obedient." But wouldn't our study, and perhaps even our application, be much richer if, like the original audience, we understood the fullness of what Jesus was saying? For example, why did He choose to contrast Tyre and Sidon with Chorazin and Bethsaida? What are sackcloth and ashes? What day of judgment is Jesus talking about?

What might we find if we looked up these cities in a Bible atlas? We would learn that Chorazin and Bethsaida are near the Sea of Galilee. We would likely find maps of Jesus' travels which would show us that Jesus spent considerable amounts of his ministry in these areas. In the Holman Bible Atlas, a map of Jesus' ministry around the Sea of Galilee lists some notes that may even surprise us as we learn that many of Jesus' disciples were from the area around Chorazin and Bethsaida, and that the miracle of feeding of the five thousand took place just outside of Bethsaida.[16]

We might also learn from maps that Tyre and Sidon were port cities on the Mediterranean. Because of their location, they were probably very important economically and well known. Turning next to a background commentary, we would discover that indeed Tyre and Sidon were important commercial centers.[17] We would also discover that they were Gentile cities with a reputation for worshiping false gods.[18]

---

16 "Map 108: The Ministry of Jesus Around the Sea of Galilee." *The Holman Bible Atlas: A Complete Guide To The Expansive Geography of Biblical History.* Nashville, TN: Broadman & Holman, 1998. 221. Print.

17 Wilkins, Michael J. "Matthew." *Zondervan Illustrated Bible Backgrounds Commentary.* Ed. Clinton E. Arnold. Vol. 1. Grand Rapids, MI: Zondervan, 2002. 73. Print.

18 Ibid, 74

Consider what we learned with just a small bit of research. How does it impact our Bible reading? Jesus is warning and criticizing Jewish people in Galilean cities; these people were witness to many of His miracles, including the feeding of the five thousand. He is contrasting them to known idol worshippers who He says will be better off on the day of judgment! That's how the original audience would have thought about it. This would have been scandalous to them! Some of the people in Chorazin and Bethsaida certainly would have seen how dire their situation was and begun to follow Him, but many others were perhaps quite offended and would have turned angry towards Jesus if they were not already. This may explain some of the polarization among the people that later leads to His trials and crucifixion. Doesn't that add so much more to the passage?

As noted, there are still other things that may offer insight into Jesus' words in this passage. For example, what does it mean to repent in sackcloth and ashes? What is the day of judgment? Again, researching these topics will enhance our knowledge of the Bible and add to the richness of the story.

Tool #3: Historical Context or Background

We now have three interpretive tools at our disposal: Literary Context, Genre and Historical Context. From now on, these should be part of every Bible study we do,[19] and will be in the

---

[19] Please note that I said every "Bible study" we do. I'm using this term, as I have throughout the book, to describe when we sit down to "dig in" to God's Word. This is a practice we should do regularly, especially when we have questions about the text. However, I don't mean to suggest that every single time we sit down to read the Bible that we consider it what I call "Bible study." For example, I often read large portions of Scripture at one sitting (such as the book of Ruth, one of Paul's letters, or even a whole Gospel if I'm on vacation). Other times I retreat to read, pray and meditate on the Word of God. Some might even refer to the practice of *lectio divina* (though I would be cautious with the way some advocate the practice be done). I certainly

remainder of this book. As we examine our third sacred cow, we will use these new aids to help us discern the accurate meaning of the passage. The more we continue to practice them, the sooner they will become a regular part of our interpretive thinking. As golfing great Arnold Palmer reportedly said, "The more I practice, the luckier I get."[20] You see the point.

Sacred Cow – 2 Chronicles 7:14

"if my people, who are called by my name, will humble themselves and pray and seek my face and turn from their wicked ways, then I will hear from heaven, and I will forgive their sin and will heal their land." (NIV)

Reading this verse isolated on its own, it appears to be a general teaching that repentance by God's people leads to His promises of forgiveness and blessing. The verse has been used in modern times as an invocation in church prayers, as a call to start spiritual revivals and even as a mantra for God's blessing of the United States. In fact, during one of his National Day of Prayer speeches, President Reagan said this promise was the "hope of

---

remain mindful of context, genre, background, and the other tools when I'm reading, just in a different, more limited way. Likewise, when I sit down on the sea wall and read Scripture, while glancing out over the ocean, I'm not thinking so much about nuances of words or the historical developments that led to my passage. Instead, it's more like reading to praise and commune with God. I'm just loving Him. So while I'm still careful not to abuse the text, I'm not as concerned with the details in those moments. Now, if I come across something that I want more clarification on, I jot down a note (or type one into my phone) and check it out later. Hope this clarification helps.

20 I've seen this quote attributed to various people on the internet, including Arnold Palmer. It reminds me of another famous quote: "The thing about quotes on the internet is that you cannot confirm their validity." – Abraham Lincoln

America."[21] Christians often use this passage as if "people" means believers today and "land" means our country.

I noted earlier in the chapter that we need to have a good understanding of the overall Biblical narrative to aid our Bible study. There are indeed important historical events which impact the meaning of this passage. As we study it in depth, we will see the importance of knowledge of the big picture story when it comes to discovering the proper meaning.[22]

The passage comes from 2 Chronicles, a historical narrative. Recall that when interpreting this genre, we need to remember that God is the focus, not man. So in this passage we should primarily be thinking about what God is doing with His people in the grander story. What does this tell us about God? Then, secondarily we consider what the passage means for the people. What did it mean for Israel? Finally, if there is an individual component to the story, we could consider that as a possible model for our behavior.[23]

Who Is the Passage About?

Paramount to finding the meaning of this passage is discovering who "My people" includes. Is it all people? Is it all Believers? Are modern Christians being referred to here? Is it the nation of Israel? Or is this just referring to "God's specially chosen people," such as the individual people God uses as prophets?

---

[21] See www.youtube.com/watch?v=T6dy-bJgBqI

[22] In order to keep this section reasonable in length, I assume the reader is familiar with the Abrahamic and Mosaic covenants, as well as King Solomon and the Temple. For those readers who may not be, this would be a good time again to practice using those Bible dictionaries.

[23] This hierarchal method of looking at Old Testament narrative is from Walt Russell, *Playing with Fire: How the Bible Ignites Changes in Your Soul* (Colorado Springs: NavPress, 2000), 107. Print.

By doing a bit of research, we would discover that throughout the Old Testament, God refers to the people of Israel as "My people" (Ex. 3:7, 5:1, 6:7, 7:4; Lev 26:12). Exodus 3:10 gives us a clear statement when it says "My people, the sons of Israel." Thus, from both the historical context and the literary genre, we see that the reference here is to the nation of Israel, and them alone.

We should also do some general research about 2 Chronicles. Using a study Bible, or another similar source, we find that the books of Chronicles are written to the generations of Israelites who returned from exile in Babylon. The author's intention is to remind the nation of God's faithfulness. Yet, as has been the case since the induction of the Mosaic covenant,[24] that promise of blessing comes with the condition that Israel needs to remember to keep His commands.[25] We saw this as well in the last chapter in our discussion of Jeremiah. This passage in 2 Chronicles is a summation of one of the key themes present in these books, and throughout the Old Testament. God wants Israel to turn to Him.

The history recorded in the first several chapters of 2 Chronicles focuses on King Solomon's reign. In the specific context of chapter 7, Israel has recently finished building the Temple. The Temple served as a symbol of God's presence among the nation. God reaffirms His covenant with Solomon and the nation of Israel, and He consecrates the Temple.[26] But God is clear. The nation must not turn from Him. From this context we again see that 2 Chronicles 7:14 is not a verse about believers in general, but only a descriptive account of the events

---

24 Again, use your resources if you're not familiar with this.
25 See Deuteronomy chapter 28.
26 See parallel passage in 1 Kings 9:1-9.

between God and the nation of Israel with God reaffirming His covenant with Israel at that time.[27]

What Is Meant By the Land?

The passage also mentions the promised blessing of land. Some historical background research can help us here as well. This promise goes all the way back to when God promised Abraham land in Gen 13:14-17. Throughout the Old Testament history, land is a key part of the narratives. A major part of the grand story is God leading His people out of Egypt and into the Promised Land. This is followed by their conquest of that land from sinful peoples. What happens to Israel through this story? Over and over again, when they sin, they often lose land. When they repent, God restores the land. This process even seems to become tireless in the book of Judges. It's easy for us to read it and think "Come on already! Again!?" But that's the point. We see in action what happens to Israel under the Mosaic covenant. Israel sins, they lose the land. They repent, and they get it back. That's God's promise (and punishment) to the nation. The blessing of the land in this passage therefore only confirms that this is a great verse for summing up the theme of the book of Chronicles, but it is not a promise to the believer today.[28]

Diving deeper we should ask: God promises to heal their land, but from what? Is it the nation's financial disparity? Is it a spiritual healing of the other people who live throughout the land? Or perhaps the people are wasting the land's resources and

---

[27] Just so there's no misunderstanding, another caveat is necessary here. I do not mean to suggest that we shouldn't pray for our country or leaders (see 1 Timothy 2:1-4). Again, we are discussing the meaning of this passage, not what the sum of Scripture says about the issue. We'll get to that topic in the next chapter.

[28] There is simply no justification for seeing this passage as allegorical. The blessing of land is simply dirt, nothing more.

God is promising to fix it?[29] The answer can be found in the immediate context, in verse 13. God is promising to heal the land specifically from drought, famine and pestilence. The Israelites understood these as judgments from God (Lev. 26:23-26; Deut. 11:16-17; 1 Kings 8:35). They had suffered many famines due to their continued disobedience. God's purpose in these judgments was to get the people of Israel to repent (1 Kings 8:35-36). In this verse, God is reminding Solomon of the covenant He has with the people of Israel and God is promising to restore their land to how it was before they sinned if they would turn to Him, yet the promise is conditional. As one of my professors said, "There's a big "but" at the beginning of verse 19."[30]

> 19But if you turn away and forsake the decrees and commands I have given you and go off to serve other gods and worship them, 20 then I will uproot Israel from my land, which I have given them, and will reject this temple I have consecrated for my Name. I will make it a byword and an object of ridicule among all peoples. (NIV)

It is an if…then statement. *If* Israel repents, *then* God will heal the land. Verses 19-20 let them know there is another option. When God reaffirms His covenant with His people, He wants to remind them of His expectations. He wants them to live up to their side of the covenant. If they do, they will be restored and blessed, but *if not*… So this verse is a reminder to

---

29 These are three examples of how I've seen this passage misapplied using the US as the beneficiaries.

30 Biola Spring 2003, Hermeneutics with Professor Ben Shin

Israel that if they follow their covenant with God, and turn from sin, He will bless them. The promise was for Israel and it has already happened![31]

Application for the Modern Christian

Again, this passage illustrates the importance of a broader understanding of the history of Israel and God's redemptive plan for mankind. The background knowledge about the book, the purpose, the history, etc. helps us have a richer understanding of the passage.

For us, the lesson is not about land, ours or otherwise, or a country. It's about a God who loves His people so much and who desires for them to be in communion with Him. God is not promising us the prosperity of land when we repent and turn to Him. That was for Israel. He is not promising to bless modern countries. The promise was for His chosen nation and it was already fulfilled. But there is much for us to learn from this. Today, as we read this story, we can be thankful for the lessons that it teaches us about God. He is faithful. He loves His people. He desires obedience. He wants to offer blessing upon His followers.

One of the reasons that we so quickly want to apply this passage as a promise today is because the New Testament teaches very similar ideas of blessing from covenant relationship with God. Throughout the New Testament, believers are told that God desires His people to be humble and prayerful, and to turn away from sin and to seek Him. But as we have been discussing in this book, we need to look for the accurate meaning in the passage we are studying. Just because our

---

[31] Notice that people who apply this today rarely talk about the curse part of the passage.

understanding of a passage about Israel may be consistent with other teachings for the modern Christian, we still need to take care to understand and apply the passage the way the Holy Spirit intended when He worked through the human author to pen it.

God does want us to pray and be humble, just like He desired of Israel. In turn, He promises to forgive and to purify us. So if you're looking for a good verse that teaches this idea to display in your home today, consider instead 1 John 1:9. "If we confess our sins, he is faithful and just and will forgive us our sins and purify us from all unrighteousness." That is a beautiful promise for us.

Conclusion

Reading a passage of Scripture, can be like watching a scene from the middle of the movie and trying to figure out what's happening. When we study the Bible, often we need to have knowledge of the background. The more details we know, the more vivid the story becomes. Background information can impact the interpretation we arrive at, which then impacts our application. If we want to get the most out of the Word God has given us, we should take the time to investigate what's behind the passage. And then, the applications we discover from the story will glorify and gratify our God.

Questions

1. In what ways does knowledge of the historical and cultural background impact our Bible study?

2. List the types of information that might be helpful to have when searching for the accurate meaning of a passage.

3. Where could you look to find out an author's purpose for writing a book?

4. Give some examples of how the influence of our culture might affect our Bible interpretation.

5. Read Mark 3:6. Who were the Herodians? Who were the Pharisees? Use a Bible dictionary to research them. Was there any special significance to those two groups collaborating together? Give an example of what it would be like today. How does this knowledge add to your understanding of the passage?

6. Bonus Sacred Cow – Read Philippians 4:13. Consider both the literary and historical context. (Read the passages around it. Look up some background information on the Philippians, on Paul's situation at the time of writing, etc.) What is the common understanding of this passage? How have you heard it used? Does Paul mean that we can do *anything* with the strength of Christ? Is a proper application using Philippians 4:13 like the military adage "be all you can be," but through Christ? Is it about obtaining goals?

Chapter 6

What Else Does the Bible Say?

I missed class one day. Well actually I missed class lots of days, but one was particularly memorable. My sociology professor was covering some material that was not in our textbook. I should have been there, but like the normal college student who regularly mixes up his priorities, I blew off class for some social activity. I had a friend in class who told me he'd take notes for me, so I figured I'd be fine. A couple weeks went by and I started cramming for the midterm, the night before. For the first time, I opened the Xerox copies of the notes my friend had taken. As I reviewed them, I was having a hard time understanding some of the information. The notes weren't very detailed, especially in a couple of key areas. I needed help! It was too late to go see the professor. I tried reaching my friend, but had no luck. Fortunately, I belonged to a fraternity which kept pretty good files on classes, but was especially rich in material from this class.[1] I went through the records, careful not to look at the past tests (ok, maybe I peeked) and found notes on the same lecture from two other people. Though they were from

---

1 The professor happened to be one of our advisors, so nearly everyone in the fraternity took his class.

previous quarters, the lecture apparently hadn't changed. But the important part was that they had information that filled in the areas where I needed help. After reviewing the material from the other notes, I was able to understand the concepts. And from what I recall, I got an A on the test.

How is Bible study like this? The Bible is not just a book; it's a library of books, all centering around the same story. And since the entire Bible is superintended by the Holy Spirit, and He is the ultimate author, we know that the message that He communicates is consistent throughout the entire Bible. If there happens to be one area we don't understand, such as a particular verse, we can turn to other parts of the Bible to help us better understand the concept. Sometimes the Holy Spirit delivered teachings in the Bible that are very detailed on a certain topic, but other times passages contain limited information, or perhaps are even vague about a particular subject or issue. By turning to other parts of Scripture that contain more detail, we can gain insight into the original passage we were looking at. Looking to different parts of the Bible gives us a larger, more complete understanding.

The Bible Is Not Written As a "How To" Manual

While the Bible in some ways can serve as our "how to" manual on many issues, it's not organized that way.[2] There are no sections entitled "Selecting a Christian spouse" or "How to be a more loving person," or "Ideas for hiding your alcohol when your Christian friends come over." When we want to find out about a certain issue, we need to look at all the passages in the Bible that relate to the topic we're studying. Theology is the

[2] Don't forget the concerns we mentioned in previous chapters about treating parts of the Bible, especially Historical Narrative, as a "how to" manual.

same. There are no books in the Bible specifically on the attributes of God, no tell-all about angels, no book on the proper way to worship, or on how sanctification works. We get our information on these topics by looking throughout the Bible where they are addressed.[3] In fact, it may surprise you, but the word "Trinity" never appears in the Bible. It wasn't used until the late second century when scholars studying the Bible used the word to label what is described throughout the passages of Scripture. As they looked at the many passages which describe God, and the passages which talk about the Father, the Son and the Holy Spirit, the early church fathers came to the conclusion that God is three persons with one nature, and the term "Trinity" was coined to describe this.[4] But it was a review of all the relevant passages which led to the conclusion. Over emphasis on any one passage can, and has led to serious doctrinal errors.

Remember back to chapter 2 when we looked at what the Bible has to say about itself and how we are to understand it. We reviewed passages from a number of books to draw our conclusion. Recall that several of the passages were from 2 Timothy. Sometimes a particular author has something in mind, so we can get a lot of our information on a subject from one book. But we still examined the rest of Scripture to make sure we had the complete picture. Likewise, we will find that in some books or sections of the Bible, there will be more information on a topic than others. For example, if we were studying

---

3 This is referred to as Systematic Theology.

4 A more complete definition is "Within the one Being that is God, there exists eternally three coequal and coeternal persons, namely, the Father, the Son and the Holy Spirit." (White, James R. *The Forgotten Trinity*. Minneapolis, MN: Bethany House, 1998. 26. Print.) Though every word in that definition is important to the proper understanding of the Trinity, I generally like to use a simpler definition: God is three whos and one what. Dr. Suess would love it.

creation, Genesis chapter 1 is filled with material, but we wouldn't use it as our sole source for understanding creation. There are many other places we should look. Psalm 104, Isaiah 42:5, Zechariah 12:1, John 1:1-3, Romans 8:18-25 and Colossians 1:16-17 are just a few examples. It wouldn't be wise to just base our understanding of creation on a single passage. Rather, we should examine the whole of Scripture.

Finding the Information

When we need help on a passage, how do we know which other passages of the Bible we should to go to? How do we find the relevant information? As we discussed in chapter 2, commentaries are useful, but are best used as a review tool after we've studied the Scripture, to check our interpretation. For now, we just want to know how to find other relevant passages. We want to examine them to see if they can aid our understanding of the passage at hand.

There are a couple of tools that can be used for this purpose. The first is often right there in front of us. If we're studying a specific passage and want to find others which are related, many Bibles contain references which point us to important related passages. Often these references are found either in footnotes or in a separate column in the center of the page. They don't give us all the information we need, but they are a useful starting point.

Many study Bibles also contain topical indexes. We can turn to the topical index if we are looking for more Bible references on a particular subject. Topical indexes have extensive (though often not complete) lists of passages which discuss or relate to the topic we are studying.

For example, let's say you're reading through the Old Testament book of Malachi and came across verse 3:8 that discusses tithing. God says the nation is robbing Him. This might raise a number of questions for you. What is tithing? How much is it? Who's it for? Is it something I should be doing? Am I robbing God?[5] Looking in one of my study Bibles, I find that it lists a reference of Nehemiah 13:10-12. Turning to that passage I see that it relates to the concept of robbing from God, but doesn't provide much more on the act of tithing itself. To learn even more about tithing, I can look it up in a topical index, which gives me many more verses to consider. One topical index I use lists this passage in Malachi, as well as 13 others under tithing. You would be much more likely to get a larger perspective on the subject as well as have an easier time answering your questions by looking up all the passages found in the topical index.

If we still want more information, we can use the tools we discussed previously, such as Bible Dictionaries. Concordances are useful as well, and we will discuss those more in our chapter on word studies.

How Is the Bible Organized?

So if the Bible is not grouped by topic, then it must be in chronological order, right? Well, kinda-sorta, but not really. So why is it in the order we find it?

I still remember my dad letting me stay up late to watch one of my favorite comedians, Steven Wright. Early in his career he often appeared on the late night shows, but his comedy rarely

---

5 Don't forget about the important lesson of context that we learned in the last chapter. It plays an important role in the interpretation of this passage. For example, verses 1:6 and 2:1 specifically tell us who this is written to.

included anything inappropriate for a kid. One of my favorite jokes of his was "Why is the alphabet in that order? Is it because of that song?" The first time I heard it, it made me laugh 'til my gut hurt. At night in bed, it kept me up as I wondered. Why *is* it in that order? Well the answer is we don't know for sure, though there are a number of speculative ideas. Thankfully, I no longer lose any sleep over it. But while there's some debate as to the development of the order of our alphabet, there's actually a practical reason that the Bible is in the order which we find it.

I've found it's especially important in Bible study to understand its organization because often people who are new to the Bible make the assumption that it's in chronological order. I've also spoken to others who thought the books of the Bible were collected in the order which they were written. Both of these are mistaken assumptions. They may not be incredibly significant, but either misunderstanding still could potentially lead to misinterpretations of certain texts. So it's a good idea to learn at least some basic things about the Bible's organization.

The Old Testament

The first five books are Genesis, Exodus, Leviticus, Numbers and Deuteronomy. These are generally referred to as the books of the Law, or the Pentateuch. The Jewish name for these books is The Torah (which means instruction or guidance).[6] These first five books tell of the early history of Israel through the time of Moses. It is important to note that even the Pentateuch is not in chronological order. Deuteronomy, written later for the new generation, records three discourses of Moses and summarizes some of the history found

---

6 When people refer to "The Torah," it also commonly includes non-Biblical writings such as the Talmud.

in Numbers, as well as repeating some of the law from Exodus and Leviticus. It does include some additional history such as Moses' last sermon, but much of it is similar to the other books. Since it's written with a different focus to a different audience, it includes some different details.

The next section is referred to as the history books and consists of those books from Joshua to Esther. This section of books covers the time period from Israel reaching the Promised Land to just after the nation's return from Babylonian exile. Once again though, we find that while the books are mostly in chronological order, there is a great deal of repeating in the books of 1 & 2 Chronicles. Like Deuteronomy, the books of 1 & 2 Chronicles are written to a later generation and have a different purpose, or focus.[7] Additionally, the books of Esther and Ruth don't fit exactly chronologically. Ruth is about a family in the time of Judges and Esther tells the story of God's work with a woman during the time of Ezra.

Job, Psalms, Proverbs, Ecclesiastes and Song of Solomon make up the next section of the Old Testament and are referred to as the Wisdom or Poetic books. This is followed by the Major Prophets: Isaiah, Jeremiah, Lamentations, Ezekiel and Daniel. They aren't referred to as Major Prophets because they were in the military, because they were taller or even because they were more important. Rather, it just refers to the length of their books. These five books are much longer than the final twelve books of the Old Testament which are referred to as the Minor Prophets. Again, the books of the prophets are not in chronological order even within their groupings (though a few

---

[7] 1 & 2 Chronicles were written to the post-exilic nation and have more of a religious emphasis, while the books of Samuel and Kings have more of a political history emphasis.

are). The events recorded in the Minor Prophets cover different time spans, but primarily fall somewhere into the time of 2 Kings and Ezra.

A really great tip that I got from my Old Testament Bible professor was that if you want to read and understand the Old Testament "story line" of the Jewish nation, it is primarily captured in the following books: Genesis, Exodus, Numbers, Joshua, Judges, 1 & 2 Samuel, 1 & 2 Kings, Ezra and Nehemiah.[8] Reading them in that order gives you a chronological overview of about 90% of the recorded Old Testament Biblical history.[9]

The New Testament

The New Testament opens with the Gospels of Matthew, Mark, Luke and John. These books record the ministry of Jesus. While originally it was thought that these books were written in this order, most modern scholars believe that Mark is the oldest written Gospel.

The Gospels are followed by Acts, which records Christianity's early history over its first 30 years or so. About half of the letters of the New Testament were written over this time period.

The letters, or epistles, make up the next section of the New Testament. Paul's letters come first, but again, they are not placed in the order he penned them. Galatians is thought to be the oldest of his epistles and appears several books in. Rather than by date of writing, Paul's letters are grouped two ways. First, they are separated by audience. The first nine of Paul's

---

[8] David Talley, *Survey of Genesis to Malachi* Class Notes Biola University. Fall 2001.

[9] See Appendix 2 for a complete chronological overview of the Old Testament.

letters are those written to churches. The latter four are those Paul wrote to individuals, often referred to as the Pastoral Epistles. Within these groupings, the letters are sorted by length, from longest to shortest.

Length Shortest ----Longest	Pauline Epistles	
	To Churches	*To Individuals*
	Romans	1 & 2 Timothy
	1 & 2 Corinthians	Titus
	Galatians	Philemon
	Ephesians	
	Philippians	
	Colossians	
	1 & 2 Thessalonians	

The epistle of Hebrews is next, followed by the General Epistles.[10] Unlike Paul's letters and Hebrews which are named after their recipients, the General Epistles are titled according to their authors: James, 1 & 2 Peter, 1, 2 & 3 John and Jude. The last book of the New Testament is the book of Revelation. It's thought to be the last book of the Bible written, but it also stands well at the end of the New Testament because it closes with visions of the New Heaven and the New Earth.

In chronological terms, the events of the New Testament can be divided into three major parts: first, the lifetime of Jesus, from about 6 to 4 B.C., to A.D. 30 or 33;[11] second, the establishment, expansion and edification of the church, from A.D. 30 (or 33) to A.D. 62; and third, the consolidation of the church from A.D. 62 to A.D. 95.[12] As noted, the Gospel

10 Many authors include Hebrews in the General Epistles, but others believing Paul to be the author, or possibly co-author, do not.

11 Scholars debate the actual dates of Jesus' birth and crucifixion, but these are the most common.

12 Martinez, G. Ted. *Matthew – Revelation*, Biola University, Interterm, 2002.

narratives fall into the first section and discuss the events in the life, death and resurrection of Jesus Christ.[13] The book of Acts covers the next period of history. Romans, 1 & 2 Corinthians, Galatians, Philippians, Philemon, Ephesians, Colossians, 1 & 2 Thessalonians and James also each fall in the time during the expansion of the church. Finally, Hebrews, 1 & 2 Timothy, Titus, 1, 2 & 3 John, 1 & 2 Peter, Jude and Revelation each address events and audiences in the latter first century period.

Knowing how the Bible is organized will help us with our interpretation of Scripture. We will be better able to determine the larger context of our passage, as well as see how the Bible all fits together. We know that when we cross reference other passages that are to the left in our Bible, it doesn't necessarily mean that they happened earlier. Likewise, when we move to the right, it doesn't necessarily make the cross-referenced passage a newer or more important revelation.

Balancing Progressive Revelation with Historical Clarity

If we move chronologically through the Bible, it's easy to see that God's revelation to His people progresses. What was once understood only vaguely is later understood with greater clarity. Knowledge about God is enriched over time. What God makes known continues to build and take shape throughout Scripture. (Romans 16:25-26, Ephesians 3:1-6). Therefore, as a general principle, later revelation takes interpretive priority. However, when we interpret the Bible, we should use this principle carefully. Sometimes a passage which dates later may be more

---

[13] Since the Gospels don't tell us precise timing on many events, and since it is difficult sometimes to determine if an event in one Gospel is indeed the same event recorded in another Gospel, harmonies vary in their sequence. Still, Gospel harmonies can be useful for aiding our understanding of the timeline of events in the life of Jesus. See Appendix 2 for some recommended harmonies.

puzzling. In those cases, we would be wise to let the more straightforward passages aid our interpretation.

Tool #4: Using the Bible to Interpret the Bible

Our first sacred cow involved a commonly misinterpreted saying by Jesus, "The truth shall set you free." We discovered how context plays a key role in finding the accurate meaning. In chapter 4, we saw how knowing about the genre is also a useful tool to discovering a passage's meaning and significance. In the last chapter, we learned how the historical context often creates a framework which we can use to better understand the meaning. We've seen in this chapter that in addition to context and genre, looking to other passages of Scripture will also greatly help us determine what God is intending to communicate. As we now look at our fourth sacred cow, we will see all these tools applied.

Sacred Cow – Matthew 7:1

"Judge not, that you be not judged." (NKJV)

Another one of Jesus' statements that is often misunderstood is found in Matthew 7:1. Jesus says, "Do not judge, or you too will be judged" (NIV) or as the King James is often slightly misquoted "Judge not, lest ye be judged." This passage is thrown out as a rebuke so often that some observers have suggested that it is the most often quoted passage in our culture, even more often than John 3:16! But do those who quote it use it the way Jesus meant?

It is commonplace today to hear someone saying "you shouldn't judge!" or "who are you to judge!?" At least the latter implies that *someone* ought to judge, though generally the intent of the person throwing out this challenge is to suggest that no one should be judging. People also often bring up this saying of Jesus as a way to end the discussion. After all, if we can get Jesus on our side, it makes this statement all the more powerful to shut someone up and let us continue to get away with our behavior. But is Jesus really saying that another person can't declare our behavior sinful or wrong?

Let's start by considering the poor logic and inconsistent behavior that many of us have when it comes to judging by looking at an example. Several years ago, I was having a conversation over lunch with a friend I will call Carrie. She was very upset about the US going to war in Iraq. I generally try to avoid engaging in political discussions, so I just patiently listened. Carrie began criticizing President Bush for the policies in Iraq, and the war, saying that we (Americans) were pushing our values on the Iraqi people. She added that President Bush was also trying to push his religion on the Middle East. She talked about how she felt that it was terribly wrong to push one's values on someone else (of course not realizing all the while that she was trying to push hers on me). I kept quiet. That is, until she mischaracterized the Bible. Carrie said President Bush acted the way he did because, as she put it, "the Bible tells Christians to go spread their religion by war and conquering other people." When she misspoke about the Bible, as an ambassador for Christ (2 Cor. 5:20), I felt I had to at least attempt to provide her with truthful information, even if I couldn't change her view of the Bible.[14]

---

[14] By the way, you've probably also heard someone say something like "Religion is the main cause of war." But in fact, only a very, very small percentage of wars have actually been the result of religion. See "The Myth that Religion is the #1 Cause of War" at http://carm.org/religion-cause-war for an excellent overview.

In a graceful way, I asked Carrie where she got her information and told her that I believed it was misrepresentative of the truths in God's Word. She immediately said she didn't want to talk about it anymore because she believed I was judging her. I was surprised by her remark, and said, "ok, we don't have to talk about it," but I asked her permission if I could clarify two things. First, I explained that I was not judging her personally or her character, but only her ideas and arguments. I apologized if I had come across that way. Then I asked if she thought that judging was wrong. She boldly said, "Yes, of course!" to which I asked, "then what was it you were doing to President Bush?" She became very frustrated and walked out of the room.[15]

Part of what caused Carrie's frustration was that she realized she was doing the very thing she was condemning. We like to judge (even if we say we don't), but we don't want others to judge us. We want to get away with our own bad behavior while criticizing others, but not to have anyone else criticize us. We certainly don't like to be accountable. This instinctive behavior makes Jesus' words "Do not judge, or you too will be judged" ones which we can call upon anytime we want to get out of a situation. Jesus said don't judge. Don't mess with Jesus. Whether it's someone judging us, or even in a situation where we are called on to judge another person's actions, just invoking the simple phrase lets us off the hook.

The unfortunate thing is that the world's understanding of Jesus' words in Matthew 7:1 is not unlike that of many Christians. And it's mistaken.

---

[15] We quickly mended our relationship, and in fact we went to a concert a couple weeks later with our spouses. Unfortunately, she moved shortly thereafter and we lost touch and never had another opportunity to discuss religion.

What Does the Whole Passage Actually Say About Judging?

This famous passage comes from what is known as The Sermon on the Mount which is found in the book of Matthew. Recall from our discussion on genre, that the Gospels are especially challenging because they often contain genres within genres (for example, a parable within the Gospel narrative). This passage is part of a discourse given by Christ. Another interpretive challenge the Gospels pose is determining if the passage is something that Jesus intended for His specific audience or something broader for all Christians. For the sake of brevity, we will go with the understanding that Jesus intends the sermon (at least this portion) to be timeless ideals for all.[16]

The Sermon on the Mount is Jesus' longest recorded sermon. Before a large crowd, He delivers a number of his moral teachings. Looking to chapter 7, verse 1, we find the passage in question. Most people just quote this verse and leave it at that. They argue that Jesus is simply saying we shouldn't judge. Period. But that's not what Jesus is telling the people. To understand the point He is making, we need to look at His entire statement, not just pull a few words out. The entire context of what is being said must be considered. Right away in verse 2, we see additional related material. Verse 2 adds that however we judge, we will also be looked at, so we should be aware. "For in the way you judge, you will be judged." (NASB) For example, when people know that we're Christians, they expect us to live by a higher standard. So, when we do something like use vulgar language, they see us as hypocrites and we do harm to the Kingdom, His Kingdom. So realize that people will judge you by

---

16 For an overview of the history of the interpretation of the Sermon on the Mount, see Blomberg, Craig. Jesus and the Gospels: An Introduction and Survey. Nashville, TN: Broadman & Holman, 1997. 244-47. Print.

your own standards of judgment. If we stopped here however, again we miss the whole of what Jesus is saying. It's not just, "don't judge and here's why." There's still more to the passage.

Notice the contrast that follows in verses 3 through 5.

> [3] Why do you look at the speck that is in your brother's eye, but do not notice the log that is in your own eye? [4] Or how can you say to your brother, 'Let me take the speck out of your eye,' and behold, the log is in your own eye? [5] You hypocrite, first take the log out of your own eye, and then you will see clearly to take the speck out of your brother's eye. (NASB)

Jesus points out that there is a speck in the eye of the person you are trying to judge, but a plank, or a log, in yours. What Jesus is saying here is not that Christians shouldn't judge. He's saying that we shouldn't judge unfairly or by a double standard. In fact, verse 5 suggests that we should then make the judgment. It says, "First" remove the log, "then…remove the speck." And if that's not enough to convince us that Jesus doesn't think judging per se is wrong, in verse 6 Jesus Himself calls the people pigs and dogs, a clear judgment on their character. Certainly Jesus isn't saying do like I say, not like I do!

So in this passage, it is clear that Jesus does not condemn all judgments, only hypocritical ones. Like the father who tells his daughter to put on something more appropriate before she goes out, but then watches porn on his computer when she leaves;[17] or the teenage girl who confronts a girlfriend about "talking

---

17 Thanks to Eric Bargerhuff for this example. Bargerhuff, Eric J. *The Most Misused Verses in the Bible: Surprising Ways God's Word Is Misunderstood.* Minneapolis, MN: Bethany House, 2012. 28.

behind her back" and then walks away and agrees with her other friend who says "she's a snob," we need to remember Jesus' words here.

What Else Does the Bible Say About Judging?

Are there judgments that are appropriate then? Moreover, are there any kinds of judgments which are commanded? The Bible speaks of judging, discerning and assessing (all related concepts) on many occasions. Using tools to research related passages, and topical indexes on judging, we would discover a number of passages, many of which have been captured below.[18] From this overview of Scripture, we can see that there are types of judging that are good and commanded, as well as types that are bad and should be avoided.

What Kinds of Judgments Are Right?

Judicial, such as church discipline. Matthew 18:15-20 tells us how this process works. (We will explore this more in chapter 8.) 1 Corinthians 5:12 also points to the necessity of discernment within the church.

Judgments of false teachings. Recall many of the passages discussed in chapter 2. See also 1 John 4:1 and Matthew 7:15-16. Clearly we are to call out and correct false teaching.

Assessments of right and wrong. Hebrews 5:14 tells us that we are to discern good and evil. 1 Thessalonians 5:21 says "test everything; hold fast what is good." (ESV) Judging right and wrong is one area where Christianity really stands out from other religions. Many other world religions generally don't tell the

---

[18] I am indebted to Craig Hawkins for providing me with an outline for the basis of this section. See his ministry website at www.thecollegeoftheology.com

follower to make these types of assessments. Some religions tell followers things like ignore reality because it is an illusion. This leads to absurdities like saying there is no such thing as evil. Some religions say don't trust the facts you see in the world because they claim the world is deceiving and unrecognizable. Still others instruct members to look at the facts, but don't make your own assessments – instead trust the head of the religion to do that for you. In contrast to all of these, the Bible tells its readers to examine the world before us and to wisely make discernments (see also 1 Peter 4:1-11 and 1 Corinthians 10:15).

Moral assessments. Behavior is a sub-category of right and wrong that also requires our judgment. Paul reminds us of this in Ephesians 5:11, and Jesus in Luke 12:57 indirectly suggests the same. We need to point out immoral behavior. However, it is extremely important to see that this does not give us authority to act as if we have a sense of moral superiority over others because of their failures.[19] Don't forget the plank in our own eye! While we should be discerning, we should be careful not to fall into the trap of being judgmental. We need to know what is right and what is wrong. At the same time, we should not look down on people, because we, too, have sinned and are no better than they are. This is such a big issue in our culture that we should be especially, perhaps even overly, concerned with it. The person who may see us as judgmental today may be the person we are trying to witness to tomorrow. Therefore, we should also be cautious not make people *feel* like we are looking down at them, even if we are not.

---

[19] Copan, Paul. *True for You, but Not for Me: Deflating the Slogans That Leave Christians Speechless.* Minneapolis, MN: Bethany House, 1998. 32-34.

What Kinds of Judgments Are Wrong?

Hypocritical, arrogant or prideful judgments. Matthew 7:1-6, as we discussed above.

Judgments by appearance alone. In John 7:24, Jesus says, "Do not judge by appearances, but judge with right judgment." (ESV) Many times Jesus' emphasizes that it's what's in the heart that matters, not the appearance. The apocryphal tale of a pastor who dresses up as a homeless man only to be shunned by his congregation reminds us of the importance of this lesson today.

Judging another's motives. Many passages either imply this or have it inherently in them (see Romans 14:4, 1 Corinthians 4:3-5, or Job 1:8-11 in context of the book's overall theme). While the Bible teaches we are to be discerning regarding another person's behavior, we are to avoid going to the next step and assessing their motives. This doesn't mean we can't make determinations about their motive if we *know* it. For example, say a police officer catches someone speeding. If the officer finds their motive was fun, versus if the officer discovers they were speeding to the hospital because a baby was being born, there is an assessment made on the motive. A ticket may or may not be issued. That kind of assessment is not condemned in the Bible. Determining whether a known motive is right or wrong is more like a moral assessment, which is commanded. Instead, what the Bible teaches is don't make guesses or assumptions if you don't know the motive. This kind of judging often causes us pain. For example, I heard a story of some people who were very worried about a person not cashing a check from an inheritance. They thought the person was going to challenge the will. They stressed and strained over it. Then, the check was eventually cashed a couple weeks later. Perhaps the individual just didn't have time to get to a bank. Perhaps the bank placed a hold on the deposit.

Perhaps the check was late in the mail. Perhaps the person was on vacation. The point is that it was needless stress by worrying over someone else's motive. There's even a great historical example recorded in the Bible where judging other's motives almost led to a civil war among the Israelites (Joshua 22:1-34). Finally, another concern with judging another's motives is that it can lead to gossip. Instead of asking someone when we are concerned about something, often we go to someone else and say, "do you think they are _____?" That's gossip. So follow the Scripture's teachings and avoid judging someone else's motives.

Judging Judging

Surveying the concept of judging throughout the Bible shows us that judging in general is not wrong. In fact, proper judgment is essential, and even commanded. Does judgment cause division? Yes. It divides truth from error. But that's a good thing. Many stories in the Bible are imperfect followers of God instructing others how to be more obedient, loving and Christlike. That's exactly what Jesus' disciples did too. They knew they were broken people, but they still spoke the truth in love. A great irony of the common misunderstanding of Matthew 7:1 is that the person saying "You shouldn't judge" actually winds up being like the one Jesus describes with the plank in the eye. They are being judgmental about not judging while judging someone else for judging. (Say that three times fast. Then say it three times slow so you can figure it out.)

Conclusion

The principle of examining other passages of Scripture to help with our interpretation is a valuable one. We've seen in this chapter how it can give us a much more complete picture of the concept of judging. It is a useful device for discerning meaning in many challenging passages. Whether you just want some additional information to help you interpret a simple passage or you're tackling something as difficult as free will and predestination, remembering to use the Bible to interpret the Bible is a valuable asset.

Questions

1. What are some advantages and disadvantages to reading the Bible in chronological order?

2. How does reading multiple passages about the same topic help us arrive at a better interpretation?

3. Use your Bible references or a topical index to find and discuss other passages which relate to judging. Do any of those passages help clarify those mentioned in the chapter?

4. In Matthew 22:39, Jesus says we are to love our neighbor as ourselves. What does He mean by "as we love ourselves"? Is He teaching that we should have a love of self here? Examine other passages about self-love to determine what Jesus means. (Definitely look at 2 Timothy 3:1-3, Matthew 7:12 and 2 Corinthians 5:14-15.)

5. Discuss the meaning of James 2:17 "So also faith by itself, if it does not have works, is dead." (ESV) Be sure to look up Ephesians 2:8-9.

Chapter 7

Word Up

"It depends upon what the meaning of the word 'is' is."[1] – President William Jefferson Clinton

As much as this infamous statement was poked fun of by the late night talk shows, it demonstrates a truth about language. Many words have more than just a single specific meaning. Instead, they have a range of meaning. As President Clinton went on to explain in his testimony, the specific meaning depends on the context in which the word is used.[2]

Some of us may still laugh at his statement, but the irony is we actually have a debate within Christianity that depends upon

---

1 http://news.bbc.co.uk/onthisday/hi/dates/stories/september/21/newsid_2525000/2525339.stm and http://www.youtube.com/watch?v=j4XT-l-_3y0

2 It was argued that President Clinton was attempting to hide the truth with a little word art by exploiting the range of meaning of the word "is," specifically its tense. Clinton was asked about a statement previously made by his attorney regarding Clinton's relationship with Monica Lewinsky. The investigators argued that Clinton's attorney lied in a previous statement when he said that there is "no sex of any kind in any manner, shape or form" between Clinton and Lewinsky. Clinton suggested that his attorney understood the question to be referring to the condition of the relationship at the immediate time of the question (as opposed to a past relationship). Whether he was misleading or not, he was correct; it depends on what the meaning of "is" is.

what the meaning of the word "is" is. When Jesus was having His final meal with the disciples, he introduced the Eucharist, or what's referred to in many Protestant denominations as the Lord's Supper or Holy Communion. It's the taking of the bread and wine. Jesus, speaking of the bread, says, "This is my body" and of the wine, "This is my blood" (1 Cor. 11:23-26). Besides His statements leading some early naysayers to call Christians cannibals, even today Christians debate Jesus' meaning among themselves. Most Catholics believe that before it is eaten, the bread and wine actually become the body and blood of Jesus,[3] a very literal view of the word "is." Many Baptists and non-denominational churches treat the bread and wine strictly as a symbolic act of remembrance of Christ's sacrifice. In this view, "is" is interpreted figuratively. Still, others see something in between where "the bread and wine are not transformed into the actual body and blood of Christ, but that the flesh and blood coexist" with the actual bread and wine.[4]

Certainly to arrive at these positions, the whole of Scripture is used, but much of it depends on the meaning of the word "is." When Jesus spoke of the bread and wine, he only used the Greek verb *esti* (English "to be"). Had Jesus been more detailed about what actually happens during Communion, there would be no need for debate.[5] Sometimes we might wish that God had been much clearer about everything in His Word. I know I do. But it's precisely that lack of total clarity that drives us to dive deeper into the text. So perhaps that's one of God's purposes

---

[3] The theological term is transubstantiation and is much more complex than the simple treatment here allows for.

[4] The theological term is consubstantiation. Miethe, Terry L. "Consubstantiation." *The Compact Dictionary of Doctrinal Words*. Minneapolis, MN: Bethany House, 1988. 62-63. Print.

[5] To dive fully into the topic of Holy Communion goes well beyond word study. A number of good references are available.

behind the way He constructed Scripture. And thankfully He didn't leave us with a Bible so big that we need a wheelbarrow to carry it around. Instead, when we are unsure of the meaning of words, we work to determine what they mean in their context.[6]

The point from this example is that words have a range of meaning. The range is often what creates differences among Bible interpretations. Spending the time and effort to discover the author's specific intended meaning of a word will many times help us to determine the meaning of a whole passage.[7]

Range of Meaning

As we learned back in chapter 1, translation is often difficult for a number of reasons. One issue that we briefly touched on was the difficulty translators face in finding the right word because words in one language often don't match up with words in another language. Instead what we find is that words have a range of meaning. Take for example the word pit. It can mean the hole in the ground where you fell, that thing at the center of the peach you just ate or where the cars are stopping to refuel in the race you're watching. Likewise, the word fast has over 30 definitions in English.[8] Many of them are used in English Bible translations. The ESV translation, for example, uses "fast" in a number of different ways: "For he held *fast* [securely] to the LORD. He did not depart from following him" (2 Kings 18:6a); "But Jonah had gone down into the inner part of the ship and had lain down and was *fast* [sound] asleep" (Jonah 1:5b); "The

---

6 Recall our discussion of 2 Timothy 2:15.

7 As you're probably figuring out, the whole process sometimes works like a spiral. Discovering meaning of the words helps us better understand the meaning of the passage, which helps us better understand the meaning of the words, etc.

8 "fast." *Dictionary.com* Unabridged. Random House, Inc. 03 Apr. 2013. <Dictionary.com http://dictionary.reference.com/browse/fast>. Web.

great day of the LORD is near, near and hastening *fast* [quickly]" (Zephaniah 1:14a); "you have established the earth, and it stands *fast* [endures]" (Psalm 119:90b); and "Then I proclaimed a *fast* [abstinence from food] there, at the river Ahava, that we might humble ourselves before our God" (Ezra 8:21a). The same English word used five different ways, with five different meanings. But remember, we are trying to discover what the original Bible author meant, and they didn't write in English. In fact, the words translated "fast" in these passages are actually five *different* Hebrew words: *dabaq, radam, maher, `amad ,and tsowm.* To further complicate matters, each of these words has their own range of meaning in Hebrew. For example, the word *dabaq,* in addition to fast or securely, can also mean "to be joined," "to pursue" or "to overtake."

It's the area where the words have common meaning that allows translation, but because of there is a range, translators sometimes choose different words.

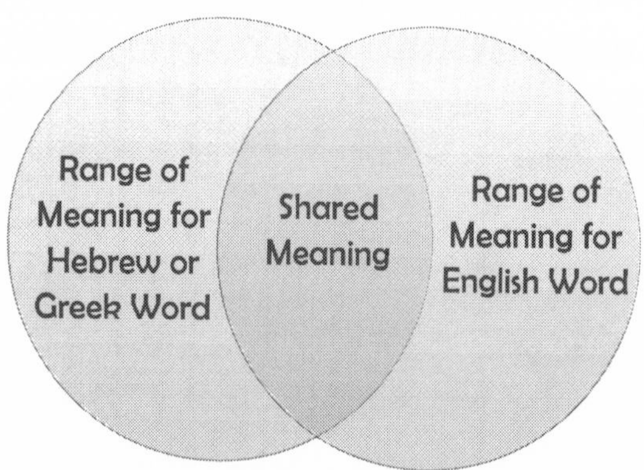

Looking at multiple translations of the same passage can help us get a better sense of the original Hebrew, but sometimes when we're trying to figure out what a passage means, the best thing to do is a more detailed word study.

One of the benefits of all the work that has gone into Bible translation is that today we don't have to know Hebrew or Greek to be able to do a detailed word study. Many excellent Hebrew and Greek dictionaries are available to help us in this endeavor.[9] Furthermore, with the availability of these dictionaries on the internet today, researching words is a snap.

Tools for Word Study

One important tool for word study is a concordance. These reference books contain an alphabetical index of all the words used in a specific Bible translation. So, a King James concordance contains all of the English words used in the King James translation in alphabetical order. *Strong's Exhaustive Concordance of the Bible* is the standard concordance for the KJV. Under each word entry, all the verses that contain a particular word are listed. For example, if we were to look up the word "foul" we would find the following entry:[10]

FOUL {5}

My face is *f* with weeping, and on....	Job 16:16	2560
but ye must *f* the residue with........	Eze 34:18	7515
it will be *f* weather today...............	Mt 16:3	5494
together, he rebuked the *f* spirit......	Mk 9:25	169
and the hold of every *f* spirit..........	Rev 18:2	169

The number in braces {} is the number of times the word appears in the translation. Each usage is listed with the verse

[9] See Appendix 1 for some recommendations.

[10] Strong, James. "Foul." *The New Strong's Expanded Exhaustive Concordance of the Bible.* Nashville, TN: Thomas Nelson, 2010. 286. Print.

reference and for each usage there is a piece of the verse included to give you a basic idea of how the word is used in that instance. Finally, the number in the last column refers to the number assigned to the original Hebrew or Greek word in the dictionary, in this case *Strong's Dictionary*. Since many people who are using a concordance don't know the ancient languages, a number is assigned to each Hebrew and Greek word for easy reference.

A dictionary, or lexicon,[11] is our other vital tool for word study. So if we want to see the entire range of meaning for the Hebrew word translated "foul" in Job 16:6, we would turn to word number 2560 in our Hebrew lexicon and find a more detailed definition.

Notice that there are different Hebrew and Greek words that were translated into the English word "foul." Again, that's because there is a range of meaning for the Hebrew and Greek words. Word 169 is translated "unclean" in other passages, while 5494 is translated "winter" or "tempest" in its other occurrences.

Welcome to the 21st Century

This process no doubt paid great dividends for those who painstakingly went through volumes of books regularly in their Bible study. Today, however, we are extremely fortunate to have computers which make this process incredibly simple. Bible software and websites are available and allow us to do word searches with just a couple clicks. One such website is blueletterbible.org. Searches can quickly be done with a number

---

[11] Lexicon is pretty much just a fancy term that theologians use for dictionary. (There are some differences, but for our purposes, just note that lexicon is the more common term used in theology. They are often more detailed than a standard English dictionary.) From this point forward, I will use the term lexicon when referring to Hebrew and Greek dictionaries.

of translations. From the home page we have many options. We can enter a word and search all its uses in a number of translations. We can see where and how it is used in specific verses. And much, much more.

Completing an English word search (as easy as putting a word in the box and pressing enter) gives us a list of all the passages the word appears in. From the list we can click on any of the listed passages for more information. We also find a link which gives us each Hebrew or Greek word in the passage along with its Strong's number. In a matter of seconds, we have a ton of information on our word. Then to top it off, with a quick click on Strong's number next to the word, it takes us to a page which includes a more detailed definition (the range of meaning) of the word. Even if this paragraph sounds complicated, trust me, it really is extremely simple. Stop here and go try it out.

Alternatively, on the same website, and others like it, you can read several translations with the Strong's number superscripted after the words in the text. An example from the NASB looks like this:

> In the beginning[7225] God[430] created[1254] the heavens[8064] and the earth.[776]

Any time you feel like you need more information about a word, just click on the number and it takes you to a detailed page. Another website, biblestudytools.com, offers the same ability to read the Bible and do quick word studies when you want. Instead of listing the Strong's number above, their website allows you to click on the words themselves, which then takes you to the original language definition page. It really is remarkable how simple computers have made Bible word search.

Finally, Bible software programs step it up by allowing you to use additional and more detailed lexicons. Depending on how much you invest, you can potentially have an incredible library of all the best word study tools. But if you don't have a Bible software program and you do plan on doing more in depth word searches using an internet based tool, it's a good idea to invest in at least one additional Hebrew and Greek lexicon.[12]

Words to Word Study

How do we decide which of the words in a passage are words we should do a word study on? The answer depends on a number of things, including how much time we have, what our purpose in the study is and how deep and wide we want to go. If you're teaching on a passage, it might be a good idea to at least briefly look up each word to get a basic understanding. You might get asked by one of your students.[13] On the other hand, if we're reading the book of Psalms in a peaceful garden on a quiet afternoon, then we *might* jot down a word or two for looking up later. Most of the time though, for general Bible study or personal journaling on a passage, we're going to want to look up at least a few key words. So what's a key word? For each reader, depending on your level of familiarity with the text, it's going to be a little different, but here are some general guidelines for determining words to research.

Theological Words

Certainly if there are any theological terms that you don't understand, take the time to do some research on those words.

---

[12] Again, recommendations can be found in Appendix 1.

[13] It seems like every time I don't do this, inevitably I get asked. Also note that teachers should be extra careful when they're teaching about the Word. (James 3:1)

Words like propitiation, sanctify, covenant and other theological terms should be well understood before attempting to interpret passages which contain them. Still, even if you think you understand the theological term, take the time to examine the word in the given context. Many times those terms carry a broader meaning than the author is intending in the particular passage.

Words that Impact Meaning

This may be a bit subjective, but be sure to look up words that appear important or seem to be significant to the interpretation of the passage. Consider researching the main nouns and/or verbs in the passage.

Repeated Words; Synonyms and Antonyms

Look for words that are repeated in a passage. Repeating words obviously indicates that an author is placing emphasis on those words. Additionally, sometimes an author uses similar words to clarify his point. They might say the same thing, but in different ways to help make their idea clear. Other times, antonyms are used to contrast ideas or to express larger meanings. All of these are methods employed by authors to emphasize points.

Figures of Speech or Idioms[14]

The Bible often uses idioms. As we discussed in chapter 1, some translations use the original idiom, while others use what

---

[14] This may require other tools besides the concordance and lexicon, because depending on the depth of your dictionary, it may or may not include information on the idiom usage.

the idiom means. If you're using a more formal translation, make sure you understand the idiom correctly by doing some additional word study.

Words or Phrases Which Are Unclear or Confusing

Like the theological terms, if any other words or phrases are unclear, spend the additional time researching them. If you don't know what an ephod, cubit or threshing floor is, look them up.

Names

Names usually don't help you to interpret a passage, but often they can add to it. For example, in the story of Jesus' crucifixion, the criminal *Barabbas* is chosen by the people to be released while Jesus is sent to the cross. The name Barabbas means "the son of the father." Thus, the son of the father is rejected for the Son of the Father. This fascinating irony is not seen by a modern English reader.

Rare Words

Finally, if we come across rare words, they deserve a bit more time. We're not referring here to rare English words, but rather to rare Hebrew or Greek words. Recall that when we do our initial English word look up, many of the tools show us all the passages where that Biblical word appears. Once in a while we'll find a word that only appears in the passage we're studying. The term for a word like this is *hapax legomenon,* meaning "being said once." If we find one of these words, extra care should be given to make sure that we understand the meaning of the term in the passage, especially if it can have an impact on the meaning of the overall passage. Plus, it's fun to tell someone you learned a *hapax legomenon.* Well at least it is for Bible nerds.

How Does the Process Work?

Once we decide which words to examine in more detail, what's next? First, if the word is a theological or ancient cultural term, start by using a Bible dictionary to get a better understanding of the concept or term before moving on to more in depth word study. Sometimes that's all we may need.[15] Other times, we will need to perform a more thorough word study. For those situations, follow the steps below.

> *Step 1* – Look up the English word (or words) in question and determine their Hebrew or Greek originals. In a word study, we are trying to understand what the author meant, so we need to study the original Hebrew or Greek word. Use a Bible with Strong's numbers, or simply go to the web and use one of the tools we just discussed. (Remember, dictionary.com isn't a website that should ever be used to develop insights into a Biblical passage.[16])
>
> *Step 2* – Determine the range of meaning of the Hebrew or Greek word. Once we find the term, we learn the different meanings the word can have. Use lexicons to gain a better understanding of the different uses of the term.

---

15 Recall the comment above about being careful to study theological terms in their context.

16 This should be clear now, but just to be sure, understand that the issue is that the English word often carries some meanings that don't overlap the scope of meaning of the original Hebrew or Greek word.

Step 3 – Ask yourself which meaning makes the most sense in the given context. Every day when we speak and use words, we primarily determine what they mean by the conversation or context. If we say, "Let's run to the store," what are we talking about? Getting groceries or exercising? Start by looking specifically at the pericope, then moving outward. Consider the following in order of priority: (1) the immediate context; (2) the author's use of the word in other parts of the current book;[17] (3) the author's use of the word in other books; (4) the use of the word by other Biblical authors; and finally (5) non-Biblical use of the term.

Step 4 – Once we have determined the meaning, it is a good idea to consult commentaries or other sources to check our conclusions.

Word Study Cautions

Doing word study is an extremely worthwhile endeavor, but it can be improperly used. If we're not careful, it can lead us to the wrong conclusions about words, and ultimately the wrong meaning of a passage.

One of the most common errors is called the root fallacy. This mistake is assuming that the roots of a word make up the meaning of the total conjugate.[18] For example, a butterfly is not a

[17] Examining the author's use of the same word in other instances can provide insight into their intended meaning in the passage being studied, but note, as this note demonstrates, sometimes authors use the same word in two different ways, even in close proximity.

[18] This is a common mistake because lexicons always lists the root, and people see an illustration to their point, so they inappropriately attach the relationship.

fly that feeds on butter. Occasionally, this does actually work. For example, the roots of the word pantheism, *pan-* and *theos*, mean all and god respectively, and pantheism is the belief that all is god.[19] But often the root has nothing to do with the word. For example, the word "nice" stems from the Latin word *nescius* which means ignorant.[20] However, even if the root of a word has some relation to the modern word, we should be cautious before we use the roots to help us determine the meaning. Knowing the root just tells us information about the history and evolution of the word. In fact, even though there are some examples where it can help,[21] the root almost never tells us what a word means in a specific context.[22] So even if it makes a fanciful illustration in a sermon or talk, be careful before interpreting Biblical words by their roots.

While step 2 of the word study process tells us to consider all the alternative meanings of the Greek and/or Hebrew words, we need to be careful not to make another common mistake, the mistake of incorporating all the possible meanings into a word. Some of us have likely heard sermons or talks where the speaker spent ten minutes or more fleshing out the total range of meaning of a word and then injected all of that meaning into a passage as if the author meant such a vast amount information to be wound up in the single word. We need to be cautious of

---

19 Harper, Douglass. "Pantheism." *Online Etymology Dictionary*. N.p., n.d. Web. 21 May 2013. <http://www.etymonline.com/index.php?search=pantheism>.

20 Osborne, Grant R. *The Hermeneutical Spiral: A Comprehensive Introduction to Biblical Interpretation*. Downers Grove (Ill.): InterVarsity, 1997. 69. Print.

21 Note that a *hapax legomenon* is often the exception. Recall our discussion of *theopneustos* (God-breathed). In instances where an author coins a new term, it is often based on the root words. So in those cases, the root can help determine meaning. However, over time, the word can change or develop new meanings, which is why when using roots to determine meaning, we should exercise such caution.

22 Fee, Gordon D. *New Testament Exegesis: A Handbook for Students and Pastors*. Louisville, KY: Westminster John Knox, 2002. 79. Print.

this error. In any given context, the meaning of a word is generally specific even though it has a range of meaning.

A related mistake is assuming that just because a word has one particular meaning most of the time, that it should have that same meaning every time it is used. If a word has a range of meaning, even if 90% of the time it has meaning A, it doesn't mean that it should mean A and not B in our context. As Bock clearly states "word meanings are determined by context, not word counts."[23]

There are many other potential errors.[24] A final one we should discuss here is the mistake of selective evidence or intellectual dishonesty. That's when we consciously, or even sub-consciously, choose certain information over other information. We favor a preferred definition, even when the evidence weighs against it. We do this for many reasons. We may be coming to the text with a biased opinion. We may be looking for a certain topic. Because of this, we should always be alert to our own biases when we are grappling with meaning. Be honest. Let the text say what it says.

Tool #5: Word Study

Our box of tools is finally complete! We have studied literary context, genre, historical context, using the Bible to interpret the Bible, and now word study. As we examine another "sacred cow," we will incorporate the lessons we've learned to this point to help us discover the correct meaning of the text. We will then see how significant word study can be to proper interpretation.

---

[23] Bock, Darrell L. "Preface." *The Bible Knowledge Key Word Study: The Gospels.* Colorado Springs, CO: Victor, 2002. 24. Print.

[24] For more examples, see Carson, D. A. *Exegetical Fallacies.* Grand Rapids, MI: Baker Book House, 1984. 27-64. Print.

Sacred Cow – Luke 2:7

"and she gave birth to her firstborn, a son. She wrapped him in cloths and placed him in a manger, because there was no room for them in the inn." (NIV '84)

The traditional church Christmas play goes something like this: Mary and Joseph have to travel to Bethlehem to be counted for the census. Mary's pregnant and so she rides a donkey on the journey. They arrive late at night and can't find a place to stay. They go to the local inn where the inn keeper tells them that he has no rooms available. The young couple is then forced to stay in a stable, where Mary gives birth to Jesus that night. The shepherds arrive and worship Jesus. The wise men show up and deliver their gifts. All is calm, all is bright. Curtain close. As we will discover here, many parts of this traditional recounting are not Biblically accurate. Take a moment now to read Luke 2:1-20 and see if you can discover some of the inaccuracies.

What did you discover? To begin with, there's no donkey noted in the Biblical story. Nor is there any mention of an innkeeper. There's also no indication that it was night when they arrived. Are you surprised? Furthermore, some of us might have kept on reading past verse 20 looking for the wise men, only to find the text telling us in verse 21 that eight days passed, and no mention of the magi. (Don't worry, we'll get to them later.) But clearly our understanding of the story seems a little different than the text.

It Came Upon a Midnight Clear

Let's now explore the passage using some of the interpretive tools we've learned so far.[25] The account comes from the Gospel of Luke. When considering this genre, recall that the primary purpose of a Gospel is to tell us about Jesus the Messiah. This thought should be in the background as we move through the interpretive process. Next, let's consider the context. Remember, in the context, we look at the verses around the verse we're examining to see if there are any clues to interpreting our verse or passage.

First though, I want to tell you a quick story about my family. My sister was pregnant last fall when she and her husband went up to visit my mom in Canada. Her husband had some contract work near where my mom lived. While they were there, my sister reached full term and had the baby, a beautiful boy that was 19 inches long and weighed 7 pounds, 2 ounces.

Ok, I confess, that didn't happen. My mom lives in Palm Desert and my sister's not even married (but she's looking, and would make a great catch). But the fake story had a purpose. When did you think the baby was born? The night they got to Canada? Doubtful. In fact, there are really just three clues that relate to the timing of the birth. The first one, "went up" suggests that for the rest of the story, they're already there. If something was going to happen at the end of their journey, the story might say "while they were on their way up" or "as they

---

[25] I draw much of my thinking in this section from Bailey, Kenneth E. "The Manger and the Inn: The Cultural Background of Luke 2:7." *Evangelical Review of Theology* 4.2 (1980): 201-17. Print. and Bailey, Kenneth E. "The Story of Jesus' Birth: Luke 2:1-20." *Jesus through Middle Eastern Eyes: Cultural Studies in the Gospels.* Downers Grove, IL: IVP Academic, 2008. 25-37. Print. See also Witherington, Ben, III. "Birth of Jesus." *Dictionary of Jesus and the Gospels.* Ed. Joel B. Green, Scot McKnight, and I. Howard. Marshall. Downers Grove, IL: InterVarsity, 1992. 69-70. Print.

were arriving." The second timing clue is "while they were there." Again, if I wanted to communicate that she had had the baby right when they got there, I might say "that night" or "when they got there," but not "while they were there." That indicates that some time has passed. And finally, she "reached full term" suggesting again a duration of time.

If you haven't already seen the connection, let me point it out. These are the exact same three timing indications in the Biblical account of Jesus' birth. So why do we think He was born on the night they arrived? The only real good answer is that it must have been the night they arrived, because we think if they had more time before the baby was born, they would have been able to find a place to stay. So we assume the birth happened that first night in Bethlehem. But again, the only timing references are "went up," "while they were there" and "the days were completed." So was Jesus born that initial night? Were they in Bethlehem for a while? Before we rush to any conclusions, let's also consider the lessons we learned regarding the importance of background information.

O Holy Night

As we noted in chapter 5, sometimes our own cultural conceptions can influence us to interpret Biblical passages differently than their author intended. The world we live in shapes our thinking and it's different than the world of the Biblical writers. Today, if a stranger knocked on the door in the middle of the night asking if they could come in, most people would probably call the police. But back then, strangers were often invited in and welcomed as guests.[26] Could our preconceptions be affecting our interpretation of this passage?

Based on what we know about the hospitality of their day, Joseph and Mary could have knocked on any door in any town and likely been invited in. Is it reasonable to assume that a man with his pregnant wife, tired at the end of a journey, would be turned away by everyone in Bethlehem? Not in that culture. Guests were to be treated generously. And the joyous birth of a child would only create the desire among the hosts to be even more hospitable. Children were considered a blessing from God. Furthermore, the text tells us *why* Joseph had to travel to Bethlehem. It was the census, which required everyone to travel *to the land of their heritage.* Surely others in his family living in Bethlehem would be expecting him, and be glad to see him.[27] Not to mention, they would get the treat of a newborn relative. The traditional story, that Joseph in the city of his family's origin, would have to seek shelter in a stable, just does not fit the culture of the day.[28]

---

[26] Barton, S. C. "Hospitality." *Dictionary of the Later New Testament & Its Developments.* Ed. Ralph P. Martin and Peter H. Davids. Downers Grove, IL: InterVarsity, 1997. 501-507. Print.

[27] It is also unlikely that the couple was alone in their travels. As we see from the story in Luke 2:43-45, Jesus' parents were traveling in a group and they didn't even realize he was gone for a whole day! People traveled in larger groups, often with other family members. That is most likely how Joseph and Mary went to Bethlehem as well.

[28] The only objection I've heard over the many times of teaching this is that perhaps Joseph's family would not want them in their home because they were not yet married (though the timing of the official marriage is also debatable) and Mary was pregnant, and that somehow that would have been scandalous. Besides the fact that nothing in the text indicates this, there are several points that should be considered. First, they do end up in a house later (Matthew 2:11). If this was an issue on the night they arrived, how come it's not later? Did the grumpy old Pharisee uncle leave? Furthermore, had this been the case, the text would likely indicate to the reader the unusual circumstances. Second, even if no other family would have them, they could have stayed with Mary's cousin Elizabeth, whom she recently visited (Luke 1:29). Elizabeth lived just outside the city in the hill country. Finally, there is still the fact that they could have knocked on many other doors in the town. Being from the line of

Away in a Manger

Ok, maybe it wasn't that night, but it was still in a stable, right? Aren't mangers in stables? And aren't stables away from the house? No one wants to smell that! Can you imagine eating a family meal with the strong aroma of manure in the air? It doesn't sound appetizing at all. Again, our cultural blinders could be concealing the correct meaning of the passage. In fact, homes back then commonly had mangers *inside* the home and there were practical reasons for this arrangement.

Kenneth Bailey spent many years living and teaching in the Middle East. In his book, *Jesus Through Middle Eastern Eyes* he offers the following comments:

> For the Western mind the word *manger* invokes the words *stable* or *barn*. But in traditional Middle Eastern villages this is not the case...simple village homes in Palestine often had but two rooms. One was exclusively for guests...The main room was a "family room" where the entire family cooked, ate, slept and lived. The end of the room next to the door, was either a few feet lower than the rest of the floor or blocked off with heavy timbers. Each night into that designated area, the family cow, donkey and a few sheep would be driven...If the family cow is hungry during the night, she can stand up and eat from the mangers cut out of the floor of the living room.[29]

King David, Joseph would have been even more notable than the average traveler. What would be scandalous is a man of his lineage in Bethlehem not being able to find shelter for his pregnant fiancée.

[29] Bailey, *Jesus Through Middle Eastern Eyes*, 28-30.

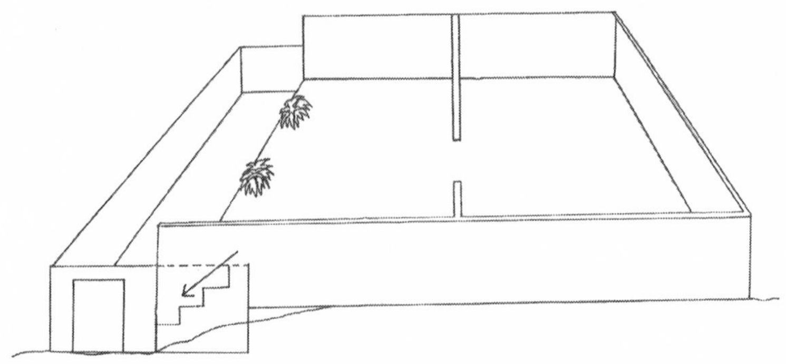

Unlike the modern home, there was no central heating. Having the animals inside the home provided the family with additional warmth. Protection of their property was the other reason animals were brought indoors. If you've ever sponsored a child or family through an international organization, you know how important a goat or another animal can be to a family. If the animal was stolen, the family could be devastated. So for warmth and to protect their animals from theft, the animals were often kept in with the family.

We Three Kings

What about the Magi that came with our nativity set? Where are they? To answer this, we turn to another of our tools: What else does the Bible say? We have additional information about the birth and infancy of Jesus from the Gospel of Matthew. Take the time now to read Matthew 1:18-2:12.

You probably noted the timing references since we've been concerned with chronology. The wise men first go see Herod. Herod then sends them on their way to look for the baby King. Some time later when the Magi arrive in Bethlehem, they find

Jesus in a stable. Wait? No, not a stable, Matthew says it's a house! Did they move?[30] Perhaps, but it's more likely, based on what we are learning, that they were already at the house.

Oh Little Town of Bethlehem

Let's review for a moment. Regarding Luke's account, neither the immediate textual context, nor what we know about the background suggests that Jesus was born in a stable the night Joseph and Mary arrived. One possible hint was the manger. But in the first century Jewish culture, a manger is equally, if not more likely, to be inside a home. From Matthew, we know when the wise men find Jesus He is definitely in a house. Everything so far is pointing to the fact that Jesus, like the average person of his day, was born in a typical Jewish home. Yet, there's still one piece that doesn't seem to make sense. Why did Luke mention a fully occupied inn? That does seem to contradict the notion that there would have been plenty of places for them to stay. At this point it's time to use our latest lesson in Bible interpretation: word study. We should investigate the word that has been translated into "inn" since it appears that that word is crucial to the interpretation of the passage.

Using a Bible reference tool,[31] we discover that the Greek word translated "inn" is *katalyma.* When we look this word up in some Greek lexicons, we find that it has several possible meanings, including "inn," "dining room" or "guest room." The

---

30 Perhaps Joseph and Mary could have moved from a stable or cave to the home at this point, but that begs the question, why didn't they just go to the home in the first place? That question has been answered above. For additional information, see the earlier footnote referring to the objection as well.

31 Reference Bibles and software programs are available for looking up words, but again I prefer to use the internet tools. Both www.blueletterbible.org and www.biblestudytools.com provide free options for this procedure.

question before us is which of those meanings does Luke intend here. As we already noted, context is the best tool for determining meaning. However, in the context of this passage, it appears that any of the meanings could possibly fit, though as we've discovered above, the likelihood of Joseph and Mary looking for an inn is doubtful. But what can we learn from our other word study principles?

Recall that the next step we should take is to find out if and how this Greek word is used in other passages in the Bible, paying special attention if it is used elsewhere by the same author, in this case, Luke. Looking up *katalyma* (in either our reference books or online), we find that the only other time it is used in the Bible is Luke 22:11 (and the parallel in Mark 14:14), where it is translated "guest room" by nearly every modern translation.[32] The passage reads "and say to the owner of the house, 'The Teacher asks: Where is the guest room, where I may eat the Passover with my disciples?'" This is from when Jesus sent Peter and John to find a room for them to celebrate the Passover. So we know that in Luke 22:11, *katalyma* should more appropriately be translated as "guest room."

Recall also that concordances can be used to look up a word in English and find all the times the English word is used in a particular translation of the Bible. To gain a better understanding of the word here, we should then also look up the word "inn" using a concordance. We discover that it appears twice in the New Testament, once in our passage, Luke 2:7, and again in Luke 10:34. Yet, from the Greek word study we just did, we know that in 10:34 Luke didn't use *katalyma* because we've already seen all of its occurrences. So let's quickly examine Luke

[32] Including the NIV, NASB, ESV, NLT, NET, HCSB. I am not aware of any translation that translates it as "inn" in this passage.

10:34. This verse is from the Parable of the Good Samaritan and reads, "He went to him and bandaged his wounds, pouring on oil and wine. Then he put the man on his own donkey, took him to an inn and took care of him." (NIV '84) Luke 10:35 also mentions an "innkeeper." This instance clearly refers to a commercial inn. By going back to our online Bible reference, we discover that the word Luke wrote here translated as "inn" is *pandocheion.* This is in fact is the normal, ordinary word for inn. If Luke (thought to be a wise physician by many) knows the common word for commercial inn, and that is what he meant as the place where there was no room in 2:7, then why didn't he use it? The answer must be that Luke didn't use *pandocheion* in the birth story because he's actually referring to a "guest room" that was occupied.

That the correct rendering of *katalyma* in Luke 2:7 is "guest room" is further evidenced by once again considering the historical background. Inns were typically only found on main roads, in larger towns. Bethlehem in that time was a podunk town off the beaten path. Without a major Roman road traveling through it, the small town most likely didn't have an inn. Furthermore, even on the off chance that it did, it's doubtful that Joseph and Mary would have had the funds to pay for lodging. As we see when they present Jesus at the Temple (Luke 2:21-40), the couple was poor (see Lev. 12:6-8). Again, why pay for a place to stay when they can knock on any door and be invited in.

Finally, we should ask ourselves if Joseph would have even considered taking Mary to a commercial inn in the first place. Inns of that day were known for their bad reputation. They were uncomfortable places where travelers were at risk of robbery or assault.[33] Would Joseph bring Mary to such a place to deliver her child? It is highly unlikely. Both the desire to have the child born in a home[34] and the poor reputation of inns would have kept that thought from his mind.

Grandma (and her interpretation) Got Run Over By a Reindeer

So it seems that the common understanding of this passage today is incorrect. The observations above lead us to the conclusion that Luke must have meant "guest room." As Bailey notes, "For more than a hundred years scholars resident in the Middle East have understood Luke 2:7 as referring to a family room with mangers cut into the floor at one end."[35] The updated 2011 translation of the NIV agrees and renders this passage "and she gave birth to her firstborn, a son. She wrapped him in cloths and placed him in a manger, because there was no guest room available for them."

Our traditional western understanding of the account is based on both a poor translation in the King James Bible, which continued for many years in western translations, and the cultural goggles that we have interpreted the story through. Careful study and research is bringing back the precision of this account, and it's starting to be reflected in western translations.[36] Still, with the cultural mythology that has developed around the

---

33 Robertson, Paul E. "Inn." *Holman Illustrated Bible Dictionary*. Ed. Chad Brand, Charles Draper, and Archie England. Nashville, TN: Holman Bible, 2003. 818. Print.

34 Bailey, *The Manger and the Inn: The Cultural Background of Luke 2:7*. 211.

35 Bailey. *Jesus Through Middle Eastern Eyes*. 31.

36 Another significant point regarding *katalyma* is that neither the Arabic nor the Syriac versions of the New Testament have ever translated *katalyma* as "inn." (Witherington, Ben, III. "Birth of Jesus." *Dictionary of Jesus and the Gospels*. p. 69.)

story, it may be many more years before it works its way into our Christmas pageants.

Joy to the World

Once, after I had just finished teaching about this, one of my friends jokingly said, "You just ruined my Christmas!" I hope you don't feel that way. On the contrary, finding truth in the Bible should only enhance the story's meaning and application for us. This story is no different.

Walt Russell, professor and author of books and articles on Biblical interpretation, reminds us that when looking for application from the Gospels, we should primarily ask "What does this passage tell us about who Jesus is and about how I should respond to being His disciple? How then should I live as a citizen of the kingdom of God?"[37]

Consider for a moment Luke's purpose in including the statement "there was no guest room available for them." Undoubtedly, it was to provide clarification to the familiar reader who reads that Jesus was placed in a manger and thinks, "The manger? That's in the front of the house. Why are they there?" And Luke explains that it was because the guest room was occupied.[38] But what does this tell us about Jesus? Why did Luke bother to mention that He was placed in a manger? Perhaps because there were people in the guest room who would not move, or were not asked to move, for His birth. Maybe they were important people. Maybe they were elderly. The point is that a hierarchy of man forced Jesus, the Savior, to be placed in a feeding trough used for animals.

---

37 Walt Russell, *Playing with Fire: How the Bible Ignites Changes in Your Soul* (Colorado Springs: NavPress, 2000), 211. Print.

38 Bailey, *The Manger and the Inn: The Cultural Background of Luke 2:7*. 212-213.

We should ask ourselves where we place Jesus in our lives. As a disciple of Christ, do I give Him the honor and respect He deserves? Or do I place worldly concerns above Him, and push Him to the less significant areas of my life?

The birth of the Messiah is joy to the world indeed. As His disciples, let's honor Him by daily remembering that He is the Lord of our lives. That means putting Him first in all things.

Conclusion

Since the Holy Spirit inspired the words, we should take care to know what He means by them. After reading through this chapter, we can appreciate how word meanings affect our understanding of a passage. Invest some time in word study. It can aid our understanding tremendously. There are many tools we can employ to help discover the right meaning of a word, which leads us to the proper understanding of the passage, which leads us to a good personal application, which brings us closer to God.

Questions

1. Go to www.blueletterbible.org or www.biblestudytools.com and use the tools to look up some Hebrew and Greek words. Also try finding all the occurrences of an English word in your favorite translation.

2. How important is it that we get our facts straight when interpreting the Bible? What do you think and why?

3. What does knowing the roots of a word offer to the understanding of the word?

4. How does context play a role in discovering which usage of a word is being conveyed?

5. Study John chapter 15. In verse 6, Jesus says, “If you do not remain in me, you are like a branch that is thrown away and withers; such branches are picked up, thrown into the fire and burned.” What does fire mean in this passage?

6. Read through Hebrews 9:11-15. In order to understand the passage better, what words would be useful to look up? (Don’t be surprised if there are many.)

Chapter 8

Bible Study

On our journey to discover how to read and apply the Bible more effectively, we've learned many important lessons. In chapter 1, we discussed the various Bible translations and how they impact our understanding of Scripture. In chapter 2, we learned the difference between meaning and significance, as well as how God helps and guides us as we read through His Word. We then spent the majority of this book learning five key tools that will aid our Bible study. Now that we have this information and these tools at our disposal, how do we go about using them?

Putting the five tools we've learned in a firm sequence is like telling a basketball team, "These are the steps to scoring…" Sure, there are going to be some common elements, like the point guard dribbling the ball down the court and the players moving into position, but for the most part, it's going to be different every time the team heads down the court. The players will need to adapt to the defense. There will be movement all over the court. Opportunities will arise. Sometimes there's passing and dribbling until the shot clock expires; other times the point guard shoots immediately. Yes, there are plans and strategies involved, but even those change as the play develops.

That's why I'm not a big fan of putting Bible interpretation into a rigid list of steps. Sometimes we skip steps, move around, jump backwards, forwards, or even start over. However, for the sake of offering a list to refer to until you're familiar with the practice of using the different tools, I've included one below – but don't get bogged down by it. Be ready to move around as necessary. Eventually, the concepts will become a regular part of your study routine and you won't need this list. But for now, this is a good order to refer to until you've become more familiar with the tools.

Steps in Bible Interpretation and Application

1. Prayer
2. General observations – Summarize the passage
3. Bible Study – What does the passage mean?
    a. Genre
    b. Context
    c. Background Information
    d. Word Study
    e. Related Passages
4. Use General Commentaries as a Check
5. Application
6. Prayer

Prayer

Studying the Word is not just a one way exercise. It's a conversation with God. The best way to begin that conversation is to go to Him in prayer. Ask the Holy Spirit to be with you and to guide you as you study the Bible. Pray that He helps illuminate the text for you. Ask that you are made more Christ-like through a conviction or personal application from the text.

To go back to the basketball analogy, prayer is like the point guard. It's the one thing that should be standard when we begin our Bible study. We should go to God in prayer first when we open the Bible to learn from His Word. Through the Holy Spirit, He will transform us with His teachings and His love.

General Observations

After you read the passage, jot down some initial impressions. What does it appear to teach? Have you heard the passage before? Do you have any preconceptions about what it means? Write down any initial questions you have about the passage. Are there any concepts you need to research in a Bible dictionary? Also note any potential words you might want to look up later in a word study.

Bible Study

Again, back to the basketball analogy, this part is where the process jumps all around. (Pun intended.) As a general rule, it's good to open by asking what genre the passage comes from. Ask how that impacts the interpretation of the passage.

Consider the context. If it's not too lengthy read through the entire book. At a minimum, find and read the broader context. Try putting your general observation of the passage through the paraphrase principle we discussed in chapter 3.

Do some background work. On certain passages we might do this step first. Jumping into interpretation without looking at the background can cause our own presuppositions to be more influential in the interpretive process rather than what was going on at the time. If we find in our initial observations that the historical context may play a large role, then perhaps we should begin there.

Do some basic research on the words you noted in your observations and follow up with more thorough work on any necessary terms. As you utilize the other tools, you may change some of the words you want to study. The larger context might reveal words that are repeated around the passage and not in the passage, yet nevertheless impact the meaning of the passage. Take more notes and look up the words you need to.

Look up related passages. Check a topical index. Use the whole of Scripture to help refine your understanding of the passage.

Use General Commentaries as a Check

To be sure that you're not totally off base, it is always wise to see how Biblical theologians have understood the passage and to check it against your findings. If the consensus sees the passage differently, you have to seriously ask yourself if you were objective and thorough in your study. Keep in mind that scholars who have put together commentaries have done much more exhaustive research into the text. Sometimes even the slightest nuance can play a large role in the meaning. Be certain that you have been true to God's Word.

Application

After you have determined the accurate meaning of a passage, look for a personal application. Often something will jump right out and hit you square between the eyes. That's likely the work of the Holy Spirit convicting you. But sometimes, finding an application might also take a bit of thinking and prayer.

Prayer

I like to end my Bible study the same way I begin it, in prayer. Sometimes this is a prayer that follows the ACTS mnemonic: Adoration, Confession, Thanksgiving and Supplication.[1] I praise God for who He is. I confess my sins, which after Bible study often includes something that was revealed to me through the text. I thank God for giving us the Scriptures to learn from and for other blessings in my life. Then finally, I ask for Him to transform me. I ask that He help me to apply the lesson(s) I learned.

One Final Example

As we go through this last example, you'll see how the process isn't always straightforward. We will move around and come back to certain points as we work to determine the correct meaning and how we should apply the text. But first, make sure you pause now and spend some time in prayer asking God to help you as you study His Word.

Matthew 18:19-20

"Again, truly I tell you that if two of you on earth agree about anything they ask for, it will be done for them by my Father in heaven. For where two or three gather in my name, there am I with them." (NIV)

---

[1] This is a good model and easy to remember, but recently I've been trying to follow the model laid out in the Lord's Prayer (Matthew 6:9-13). (1) Pray for the glory of God. (2) Pray for the Kingdom of God to be advanced. (3) Pray for the will of God. (4) Pray for the needs of this life. (5) Confess my sins. (6) Pray that I continue to strive toward holiness and for deliverance.

General Observations

This passage appears to be a promise from God that if we are gathered in prayer with other Christians and we ask something of Him, God will answer our request. On the surface, what the group can ask for appears to be wide open with the only qualification being that we agree on it. (Yes! My wife and I both agree that we want a house on the beach in Hawaii!) However, even those not very familiar with theology will realize that there are some limitations to what we can ask of God and have Him answer. By searching the rest of Scripture for related passages, we can gain some insights. For now, we can make a note that we may want to do some additional research on that subject if the passage is indeed about God answering group prayer.

Verse 20 says that if two or three people are gathered, then God is with them. I've heard this verse used at concerts and numerous times during worship at church. Perhaps you have as well. Worship leaders quote it, saying that the Bible teaches that if two or more of us are together, then God is with us. That idea does seem consistent with verse 19, but as we've seen several times, we should always examine the surrounding context.

Some other questions that come to mind: What's happening when Jesus says this? Is it at a prayer meeting? Is it at a worship service? Is it at a Rolling Stones concert?[2] What's the situation here? And what about the "two people" thing? Isn't God always with me when I'm alone? Isn't God present with Christians all the time? Is it different when there is more than one person? And Jesus said two or three – what if there are four or more? Finally, what if one group of two or three disagrees with another

---

2 What, weren't they around then?

group of two or three? How does God decide which prayer to answer?

Then, there are certainly words that should be investigated more. "Again" is one of them. Like "therefore" appearing at the beginning of a sentence,[3] "again" likely indicates that what came before it is related, unless perhaps the meaning in Greek was something different. That should be checked out. There doesn't appear to be any theologically loaded words, or other words that need to be investigated, but as is common with Bible study, many of the words to be looked up only become apparent further along into the process.

A Deeper Look

As we noted in chapter 4, genre can often give us a strong sense of how to understand a passage even before knowing its context. This passage comes from the Gospel of Matthew. As a reminder, the Gospels are filled with many other kinds of genres. In looking around this passage, we see that it appears to be historical narrative. It's a recording of Jesus' teachings. He is giving instruction on a number of issues. So, knowing this, we should ask questions like: Whom is the instruction for? Is it to the audience He's speaking to? Is it to everyone? Does it apply to Christians today? To answer these questions, we need to examine the context in more detail. Where does immediate context begin? And what is the larger context?

---

[3] I've heard this saying from a number of people. It's a good play on words that helps remind us that whenever you see "therefore" in the text, always ask "What's the 'therefore,' there for?"

Discovering the Immediate Context

The first context related question we should ask is, "Do these two verses stand alone, or are they part of a larger pericope?" To begin, let's examine the word "again." (See, we've already jumped to word study to help us with context.) Using a concordance, we discover that the Greek word is *palin.* It has a limited range of meaning. The three main options are: "anew" as in repeating the action (probably to describe the same thing in a different way); "again" as in the sense of furthermore or moreover; and "on the other hand."[4] Each of these would indicate that the context is continuing from the previous verses.[5] So let's go back and read from verse 15.

> "If your brother or sister sins, go and point out their fault, just between the two of you. If they listen to you, you have won them over. But if they will not listen, take one or two others along, so that 'every matter may be established by the testimony of two or three witnesses.' If they still refuse to listen, tell it to the church; and if they refuse to listen even to the church, treat them as you would a pagan or a tax collector. Truly I tell you, whatever you bind on earth will be bound in heaven, and whatever you loose on earth will be loosed in heaven." (NIV)

---

4 Blue Letter Bible. "Dictionary and Word Search for *palin (Strong's 3825)*". Blue Letter Bible. 1996-2013. 28 May 2013. < http:// www.blueletterbible.org/lang/lexicon/lexicon.cfm?Strongs=G3825&t=NIV >

5 Note that even if *palin* was translated "on the other hand," it still implies that the context is continuing, but instead of a furthermore, it would be a contrasting statement (see Matthew 4:7 and Luke 6:43 for this type of usage). However, this usage would make Jesus' statements quite odd because He is not contrasting, He is repeating. So *palin* is either in the sense of "moreover" or Jesus is simply rephrasing His statement in another way.

We should notice right away the reference to "take one or two others" in verse 16. One or two, plus the one taking them, equals two or three, the same phrase we find in verse 20. This also indicates there is a connection between verses 15-18 and 19-20.

There is still more evidence that the verses are part of the same pericope. Verse 19 specifically adds "on earth." This connects it to the preceding verse which says the decision "on earth" will receive the Father's blessing in Heaven. Thus, verse 19 is repeating the thought in verse 18 by saying it again in a different way. Jesus is assuring His church that God in Heaven will honor and ratify the decision made by man on earth.

The connection of these verses calls into question some of the ways we've seen this passage used. It appears that the passage is about the specific issue of church discipline, rather than God's people in general being in community. Jesus is offering His people instruction for how to handle sin when it arises among His followers. In fact, if we had chosen to review some background commentaries prior to word search, we would be being led to the same conclusion. So let's turn to them now.

Background Research

Background commentaries are useful because they can provide us with information about the historical and cultural details behind a passage. They can also help clear up misconceptions we might have when we approach the text. The Victor Bible Background Commentary clarifies that verse 19 "is not about prayer at all."[6] Rather, as the ZIBBC explains, "Jesus addresses in a practical manner what the community of disciples must do if

---

[6] Richards, Larry. *The Victor Bible Background Commentary: New Testament.* Wheaton, IL: Victor, 1994. 69. Print.

one in the family commits a sin."[7] It was the norm of the day that Jewish courts needed to have two or three witnesses to establish testimony to be true.[8] So, when Jesus refers to two or three, He is simply reinforcing a principle that the Jewish people were already familiar with.

As we are going through this interpretive process, we might look at the verses that are tied to the context (verses 15-18) and discover that a couple additional questions arise. The first is: What does it mean to treat someone as a pagan or a tax collector (verse 17)? Again, using our background commentaries, we discover that pagans and tax collectors were common terms for people who were antagonistic to God and the early Christians. So, rather than follow the Jewish practices of flogging or stoning, Jesus encourages His disciples to use a different approach when dealing with sinners who continue to be rebellious. He says to treat them as if they were outside the community.[9]

The Broader Context

Looking at a larger section of Matthew, we see that our passage is surrounded by other passages that deal with how believers are to relate to one another. Therefore, the overall context is one in which Jesus is teaching principles to His followers about how to relate to one another. The whole section is about this concept. In terms of the meaning of our specific passage, this fact stresses the importance of discipline and accountability in our relationship to other believers.

---

[7] Wilkins, Michael J. "Matthew." *Zondervan Illustrated Bible Backgrounds Commentary*. Ed. Clinton E. Arnold. Vol. 1. Grand Rapids, MI: Zondervan, 2002. 114-15. Print.

[8] Ibid, 114-115 and see also Deut. 17:2-7; 19:15-21.

[9] Ibid, 114.

An additional insight can be made when we look at the pericopes which bracket our passage. Immediately before Matthew 18:15-20 is the parable of the wandering sheep. Among other things, this parable teaches that the wandering soul is just as important to God as His other followers. And, just after the passage on church discipline, we find Peter asking Jesus how many times one should forgive a sinning brother. Jesus' answer suggests that forgiveness should be given without limitation. The bracketing of two such teachings helps show that the main intent of church discipline is not to rid the church of sinners. Instead, the primary goal of church discipline is to ultimately bring restoration and reconciliation to the believer (Galatians 6:1).

The Rest of Scripture

Based on the tools we've used so far, we should be pretty confident about our understanding of the passage, but we still haven't spent much time looking at other passages outside of the book of Matthew. One quick check we could do to help confirm our interpretation is to see if the Bible has any other occasions where it speaks of two or three together. And if so, do those passages teach that there is something special about that number of believers gathering together?

Using our web research tools, a quick study can be done for "two or three." We find that the Bible speaks of two or three witnesses together on six occasions (Deut. 17:2-7; 19:15-21; Matt. 18:15-20; 2 Cor. 13:1-4; 1 Tim. 5:17-22 and Heb. 10:26-31). What do they have in common? Each time, the two or three are mentioned in the context of dealing with sin (not prayer) among God's people. This finding supports our interpretation of this passage.

At this point, we could move on, or we might desire to expand our study. If we were really diving deep into this passage, we could do additional research on other passages that discuss which acts require church discipline. Using a topical index to look up discipline, we would find a number of passages that could be examined for further insight. We would discover that the Bible does tell us some specific sins that call for church discipline. They include sexual immorality, idolatry and being a drunkard (1 Cor. 5:1-13), as well as causing division in the church through false teaching (Titus 3:9-11).

Because of some of our initial thoughts on the passage (specifically about it being related to God being present with believers), we might also be interested in finding out more about God's omnipresence (His being everywhere at once), so we could use a topical index or Bible dictionary to look for passages which discuss this attribute. Our study can go in a number of directions and with the tools we have available to us now, we should be able to navigate through the Scriptures very effectively.

Review

Going back to examine our original questions in our general observations, we see that the questions were either answered by our study,[10] or that the question is irrelevant because our observation about the passage was mistaken. If there were any questions that still needed answering, we could continue our

---

[10] For example, even the question about what we can ask for has been clarified. The text says, when two or three ask about *anything* that it will be done. But is clear now that *anything* doesn't mean whatever we want, in any context. It means *anything* in the context of that situation. Just like if my wife asks me what I want to have for dinner, and I say "Anything is fine." I obviously don't mean I want to eat dirt. "Anything" is in the context of food that we would eat.

study. Finally, we should always examine some general commentaries and/or other resource materials to confirm the accuracy of our interpretations. After examining commentaries, we would find that the interpretation we arrived at is indeed the consensus view of Matthew 18:15-20.

In his book on Biblical interpretation Walt Russell writes,

> within these verses themselves [referring to Matt. 18:19-20], there seems to be ample support for their widespread use as either very general prayer or "presence" promises. However, a very different sense of meaning emerges when we put these verses within the context of their unit of thought...verses 19-20 bring to finality earlier points that Jesus stated in the paragraph.[11]

He adds,

> In terms of spiritual formation, too many of us wrongly claim these verses in contexts that Jesus never intended. His words are for an extremely important and extremely narrow context: church discipline.[12]

Application

In this section of Matthew's Gospel, Jesus offers us a number of principles about how we are to relate to other Christians. Among them is how to discipline a brother who has sinned. How come we so seldom follow this procedure? Perhaps because so many people misunderstand this passage. Or perhaps because church

---

[11] Walt Russell, *Playing with Fire: How the Bible Ignites Changes in Your Soul* (Colorado Springs: NavPress, 2000), 68,70. Print.

[12] Ibid, 72.

discipline involves not being "nice." Either way, it seems to be a teaching that has been neglected by the modern church. Instead of using verses 19-20 in unintended ways, we should feel privileged at the confidence God has placed in His church. Instead of being afraid of being negative, we should see this passage for what it is: a powerful tool for bringing about repentance and restoration. So one obvious way that we can apply this passage is just to start doing what it says.

Thinking back to our lesson on application from chapter two, we recall that there is only one meaning of a passage, but within the scope of that meaning, there can be multiple applications based on what the passage is teaching. Looking at Matthew 18:15-20, we can also gain insights about God's character. We always talk and sing so much about how God values us individually (which He does), but this passage also shows us how God values community. He wants the community to remain pure, and He trusts the community to make important decisions.

We also learn from this passage some things God expects of us. For example, He wants us to take some responsibility for the purity of others within the community. Certainly, there is conviction from the Holy Spirit in individuals who sin, but sometimes God desires that we participate in their process of healing.

From these insights, we could draw some personal significance. We might need to learn the importance of community so that we actively participate more, or we might know someone who is sinning that needs to be restored. That's one of the beauties of application. Just like Paul wrote to Timothy, it is so that we are thoroughly equipped to do good works (2 Timothy 3:17).

Final Thoughts

"The grass withers and the flowers fall, but the word of our God endures forever." Isaiah 40:8 (NIV)

We've reached the end of our journey, or more appropriately the beginning. While we covered a great deal of material, there's still much we didn't cover. For example: How do we interpret all of the imagery in the book of Revelation? Should we read Christ back into the Old Testament? How are we to understand passages that talk about God having a hand, or even walking places? Are the most destructive acts in the Old Testament written actually as they occurred or are they hyperbole? These are just a few of the more complex issues that you may encounter as you engage the more perplexing passages or theological issues. Some of the books recommended in the footnotes of this book and in the appendix provide much more depth if you're looking for it. But with the tools we've learned, you should be well-equipped to handle most of what you'll encounter, including some of the more challenging passages of Scripture.

The more you practice these skills, the better you'll get at them. You'll learn to ask better questions. You will recall more details of the grand story, and see how it all relates. You'll know when to use each of the tools. Your word knowledge will become more robust. And you will continue to grow as you learn to discern meaning and find application from God's eternal Word.

To get more of *Discover the Bible*, visit
http://discoverthebible.wordpress.com/

Appendix 1 – Recommended Resources

The lists below are recommended sources to help you in your Bible study. I have placed a smiley face (☺) after the materials I highly recommend that you pick up to start your library. In some of the categories, I have classified the materials (Beginning, Intermediate or Advanced) to help you decide which materials are best for your needs.

Bible Handbooks / Dictionaries / Encyclopedias

Brand, Chad Owen., Charles W. Draper, and Archie W. England. *Holman Illustrated Bible Dictionary*. Nashville, TN: Holman Bible, 2003. ☺

Dockery, David S., ed. *Holman Bible Handbook*. Nashville, TN: Holman Bible, 1992.

Holman Illustrated Bible Handbook. Nashville, TN: Holman Bible, 2012. Print. (This book is complete with QR codes that take you to the web for more information and videos. Wow!) ☺

IVP Dictionary Series. Downers Grove, IL: InterVarsity.

Bible Atlases

Beitzel, Barry J. *The New Moody Atlas of the Bible*. Chicago, IL: Moody, 2009.

Brisco, Thomas. *The Holman Bible Atlas: A Complete Guide To The Expansive Geography of Biblical History*. Nashville, TN: Broadman & Holman, 1998. ☺

Rasmussen, Carl. *Zondervan Atlas of the Bible*. Grand Rapids, MI: Zondervan, 2010.

Surveys

Archer, Gleason L. *A Survey of Old Testament Introduction.* Chicago, IL: Moody, 2007. (Intermediate)

Arnold, Bill T., and Bryan Beyer. *Encountering the Old Testament: A Christian Survey.* Grand Rapids, MI: Baker Academic, 2008. (Beginning – Intermediate)

Carson, D. A., and Douglas J. Moo. *Introducing the New Testament: A Short Guide to Its History and Message.* Grand Rapids, MI: Zondervan, 2010. (Beginning)

Carson, D. A., and Douglas J. Moo. *An Introduction to the New Testament.* Grand Rapids, MI: Zondervan, 2005. (Intermediate)

Gundry, Robert H. *A Survey of the New Testament.* 4th ed. Grand Rapids, MI: Zondervan, 2003. (Beginning – Intermediate)

Background Commentaries

Keener, Craig S. *The IVP Bible Background Commentary: New Testament.* Downers Grove, IL: InterVarsity, 1993. (Beginning – Intermediate)

Richards, Larry. *The Victor Bible Background Commentary: New Testament.* Wheaton, IL: Victor, 1994. (Beginning)

Walton, John H., Victor Harold. Matthews, and Mark W. Chavalas. *The IVP Bible Background Commentary: Old Testament.* Downers Grove, IL: InterVarsity, 2000. (Beginning – Intermediate)

Zondervan Illustrated Bible Background Commentary Set: New Testament. (Beginning – Intermediate) ☺

Zondervan Illustrated Bible Background Commentary Set: Old Testament. (Beginning – Intermediate) ☺

Book Commentary Series

Baker Exegetical Commentary. Grand Rapids, MI: Baker. (Intermediate – Advanced)

Encountering Biblical Studies. Grand Rapids, MI: Baker. (Beginning – Intermediate)

Expositor's Bible Commentary. Grand Rapids, MI: Zondervan. (Intermediate)

New International Commentary on the New Testament (NICNT). Grand Rapids, MI: Eerdmans. (Intermediate-Advanced)

New International Greek Testament Commentary (NIGTC). Grand Rapids, MI: Eerdmans. (Advanced)

NIV Application Commentary. Grand Rapids, MI: Zondervan. (Beginning – Intermediate)

Preaching the Word. Wheaton, IL: Crossway. (Beginning)

Word Biblical Commentary. Nashville, TN: Thomas Nelson. (Advanced)

Theology

Bickel, Bruce, and Stan Jantz. *Bruce & Stan's Guide to God: A User-friendly Approach.* Eugene, OR.: Harvest House, 1997. (Beginning)

Enns, Paul P. *The Moody Handbook of Theology.* Chicago, IL: Moody, 1989. (Intermediate)

Geisler, Norman L. *Systematic Theology.* Minneapolis, MN: Bethany House, 2002. (Intermediate)

Grudem, Wayne A. *Systematic Theology: An Introduction to Biblical Doctrine.* Leicester, England: Inter-Varsity, 1994. (Intermediate – Advanced) ☺

Lexicons

Arndt, William, F. Wilbur Gingrich, Frederick W. Danker, and Walter Bauer. *A Greek-English Lexicon of the New Testament and Other Early Christian Literature.* 2nd ed. Chicago: University of Chicago, 1979.

Brown, Francis, S. R. Driver, and Charles A. Briggs. *The Brown, Driver, Briggs Hebrew and English Lexicon: With an Appendix Containing the Biblical Aramaic : Coded with the Numbering System from Strong's Exhaustive Concordance of the Bible.* Peabody, MA: Hendrickson, 2001.

Harris, R. Laird, Gleason L. Archer, and Bruce K. Waltke. *Theological Wordbook of the Old Testament.* Chicago: Moody, 1980.

Websites

www.biblegateway.com
www.biblehub.com
www.biblestudytools.com
www.blueletterbible.org
www.netbible.com

Other Recommended Bible Study Resources

Archer, Gleason L. *Encyclopedia of Bible Difficulties.* Grand Rapids, MI: Zondervan Pub. House, 1982. ☺

Fee, Gordon D., and Douglas K. Stuart. *How to Read the Bible Book by Book.* Grand Rapids, MI: Zondervan, 2002. ☺

House, H. Wayne. *Chronological and Background Charts of the New Testament.* Grand Rapids, MI: Zondervan, 1981.

Strong, James. *The New Strong's Expanded Exhaustive Concordance of the Bible.* Nashville, TN: Thomas Nelson, 2010. Print. (If you prefer a hard copy to the internet.)

Thomas, Robert L. *Charts of the Gospels and the Life of Christ.* Grand Rapids, MI: Zondervan Pub. House, 2000.

Walton, John H. *Chronological and Background Charts of the Old Testament.* Grand Rapids, MI: Zondervan, 1994.

Appendix 2 – Biblical Chronology

Old Testament Chronology

<table>
<tr><th>History (Storyline)</th><th>Additional History / Side Stories</th><th>Law / Prophets</th><th>Poetry / Wisdom literature*</th><th>Other</th></tr>
<tr><td>Genesis 1</td><td></td><td></td><td>Psalm 104</td><td></td></tr>
<tr><td>Genesis 2-11</td><td>1 Chronicles 1:1-27</td><td></td><td></td><td></td></tr>
<tr><td></td><td></td><td></td><td></td><td>Job</td></tr>
<tr><td>Genesis 12-50</td><td>1 Chronicles 1:28-2:4</td><td></td><td></td><td rowspan="19">1 Chronicles 2:5 - 9:44</td></tr>
<tr><td>Exodus 1-19</td><td></td><td></td><td>Proverbs 22:17-24:34**</td></tr>
<tr><td></td><td rowspan="7">Deuteronomy</td><td>Exodus 20-31</td><td></td></tr>
<tr><td>Exodus 32-40:16</td><td></td><td></td></tr>
<tr><td>Exodus 40:17-35</td><td>Leviticus</td><td></td></tr>
<tr><td>Exodus 40:36-38</td><td></td><td></td></tr>
<tr><td>Numbers 1-13</td><td></td><td></td></tr>
<tr><td>Numbers 14-15</td><td></td><td>Psalm 90</td></tr>
<tr><td>Numbers 16-36</td><td></td><td>Psalm 91</td></tr>
<tr><td>Joshua</td><td></td><td></td><td></td></tr>
<tr><td>Judges 1:1-5:31</td><td></td><td></td><td></td></tr>
<tr><td>Judges 6:1-9:57</td><td>Ruth***</td><td></td><td></td></tr>
<tr><td>Judges 10:1-21:25</td><td></td><td></td><td></td></tr>
<tr><td>1 Samuel 1-17</td><td></td><td></td><td></td></tr>
<tr><td>1 Samuel 18-20</td><td></td><td></td><td>Psalms 11, 59</td></tr>
<tr><td>1 Samuel 21-24</td><td></td><td></td><td>Ps. 7, 27, 31, 34, 52, 56, 120, 140-142</td></tr>
<tr><td>1 Samuel 25-27</td><td></td><td></td><td>Psalms 17, 35, 54, 63</td></tr>
<tr><td>1 Samuel 28-30</td><td></td><td></td><td>Ps. 121, 123-125, 128-130</td></tr>
<tr><td>1 Samuel 31</td><td>1 Chronicles 10</td><td></td><td></td></tr>
</table>

2 Samuel 1-4			Ps. 6, 8-10, 14, 16, 19, 21, 43-45, 49, 73, 77-78, 81, 84-84, 87-88, 92-93	
2 Samuel 5:1-10	1 Chronicles 11:1-9		Ps. 102-103, 106-107, 133	
2 Samuel 5:11-25	1 Chronicles 14		Ps. 1-2, 15, 22-24, 47, 68, 89, 100-101	
2 Samuel 6:1-11	1 Chronicles 13			
2 Samuel 6:12-19a	1 Chronicles 15:1-16:3			
1 Chronicles 16:4-42			Psalms 96, 105, 106	
2 Samuel 6:19b-23	1 Chronicles 16:43		Ps. 25, 29, 33, 36, 39, 50, 53, 60, 75	
2 Samuel 7-8	1 Chronicles 17-18			
2 Samuel 9				
2 Samuel 10:1-11:1	1 Chronicles 19:1-20:1a		Ps. 20, 65-67, 69-70	
2 Samuel 11:2-12:25			Ps. 32, 51,86, 122	
2 Samuel 12:26-31	1 Chronicles 20:1b-3			
2 Samuel 13:1-21:14			Ps. 3-5, 12-13, 26, 28, 38, 40-42, 55, 58, 61-62, 64	
2 Samuel 21:15-22	1 Chronicles 20:4-8		Psalm 57	
2 Samuel 22			Psalm 18	
2 Samuel 23:1-7			Psalms 95, 97-99	
2 Samuel 23:8-39	1 Chronicles 11:10-47			
1 Chronicles 12				
2 Samuel 24	1 Chronicles 21:1-22:1		Psalms 30, 108-110	
1 Kings 1:1-2:9				

1 Chronicles 22:2-29:22a			Psalms 111-118, 127, 131, 138-139, 143-145	
1 Kings 2:10-12	1 Chronicles 29:22b-30		Psalms 37, 71-72, 94, 119	
1 Kings 2:13-46a				
1 Kings 2:46b-3:15	2 Chronicles 1:1-13		Proverbs 1:1 - 22:16, 25:1 - 29:27	
1 Kings 3:16-4:19				
1 Kings 4:20-21	2 Chronicles 9:26			
1 Kings 4:22-34				
1 Kings 5:1-7:51	2 Chronicles 2:1-5:1			
1 Kings 8	2 Chronicles 5:2-7:10		Ecclesiastes, Song of Solomon, Ps. 132, 134, 136, 146-150	
1 Kings 9	2 Chronicles 7:11-8:18			
1 Kings 10, 4:21	2 Chronicles 9, 1:14-17			
1 Kings 11:1 - 12:24	2 Chronicles 9:29-11:4			
1 Kings 12:25-33				
2 Chronicles 11:5-23				
1 Kings 13:1-14:20				
1 Kings 14:21-15:6	2 Chronicles 12:1-13:2			
2 Chronicles 12:3-21				
1 Kings 15:7-12	2 Chronicles 13:22-14:5			
2 Chronicles 14:6-15:15				
1 Kings 15:13-15:24	2 Chronicles 15:16-17:1			
1 Kings 15:25-21:29			Proverbs 30, 31	
2 Chronicles 17				
1 Kings 22:1-40	2 Chronicles 18			
2 Chronicles 19:1-20:30			Psalms 82-83	

1 Kings 22:41-50	2 Chronicles 20:31-21:1			
1 Kings 22:51 - 2 Kings 8:15				
2 Kings 8:16-22	2 Chronicles 21:2-10			
2 Chronicles 21:11-17				
2 Kings 8:23-29	2 Chronicles 21:18-22:6			
2 Kings 9:1-13				
2 Kings 9:14-29	2 Chronicles 22:7,9			
2 Kings 9:30-10:11				
2 Kings 10:12-14	2 Chronicles 22:8			
2 Kings 10:15-36				
2 Kings 11:1-12:16	2 Chronicles 22:10-24:14			
2 Chronicles 24:15-22				
2 Kings 12:17-21	2 Chronicles 24:23-27			
2 Kings 13				
2 Kings 14:1-22	2 Chronicles 25:1-26:2			
2 Kings 14:23-29				
2 Kings 15:1-3	2 Chronicles 26:3-5	Jonah		
2 Chronicles 26:6-15				
2 Kings 15:4-7	2 Chronicles 26:16-23	Isaiah 1-8		
2 Kings 15:8-31		Amos		
2 Kings 15:32-16:5	2 Chronicles 27:1-28:7			
2 Chronicles 28:8-15				
2 Kings 16:6-20	2 Chronicles28:16-27	Isaiah 9-27, Micah, Hosea		
2 Kings 17				
2 Kings 18:1-3	2 Chronicles 29:1-2			
2 Chronicles 29:3-30:27			Psalm 48	

2 Kings 18:4-8	2 Chronicles 31:1			
2 Chronicles 31:2-21		Isaiah 28-35		
2 Kings 18:9-12				
2 Kings 18:13-37	2 Chronicles 32:1-19	Isaiah 36		
2 Kings 19	2 Chronicles 32:20-23	Isaiah 37	Psalms 76, 46, 80, 135	
2 Kings 20:1-11	2 Chronicles 32:24-26	Isaiah 38		
2 Chronicles 32:27-30				
2 Kings 20:12-19	2 Chronicles 32:31	Isaiah 39-66		
2 Kings 20:20-21:26	2 Chronicles 32:32-33:25	Nahum		
2 Kings 22:1-24:20	2 Chronicles 34:1-36:21	Zephaniah		
2 Kings 25		Jeremiah	Psalms 74, 79	
		Habakkuk, Lamentations, Ezekiel, Daniel		
Ezra 1:1-4	2 Chronicles 36:22-23			
Ezra 1:5-6:22		Haggai, Zechariah, Joel, Obadiah****	Psalm 137	
	Esther			
Ezra 7-10				
Nehemiah		Malachi	Psalm 126	

NOTE: The dating of many of these books and passages is debated, and the above references do not necessarily reflect my view. This table is provided to help the reader orient the events of the Old Testament, as well as for a suggested reading plan.

* Some of the Psalms do not refer directly to specific events, but rather themes, therefore could fit in several places. Others, however, are directly related to specific events of history.

** See Expositor's Bible Commentary for reasons for this pre-Solomon dating.
*** Some place the book of Ruth later in Judges, primarily because there are only three generations listed until David. However, there are other historical reasons to place it here.
**** The dates of both Joel and Obadiah are debated and may be much earlier.

Chart References

"Daily Bible Reading: Chronological Plan." *Blue Letter Bible.* Web. 22 Sept. 2009.

Newsome, James D. *A Synoptic Harmony of Samuel, Kings, and Chronicles: With Related Passages from Psalms, Isaiah, Jeremiah, and Ezra.* Eugene, Or.: Wipf and Stock, 2002. Print.

Ross, Allen P. "Proverbs." *The Expositor's Bible Commentary: With the New International Version of the Holy Bible, Psalms, Proverbs, Ecclesiastes, Song of Songs.* Ed. Frank E. Gaebelein. Grand Rapids: Zondervan Pub. House, 1991. 881-1134. Print.

Talley, David. *Survey of Genesis to Malachi* Class Notes Biola University. Fall 2001.

The New Open Bible: Study Edition. Nashville, TN: Thomas Nelson, 1990. Print.

Walton, John H. *Chronological and Background Charts of the Old Testament.* Grand Rapids, MI: Zondervan, 1994. 12, 26-27. Print.

Gospel Chronology

My favorite Gospel harmony is by Orville Daniel. The best thing about this harmony is that it offers the reader a story line that they can read which intertwines the text of all four Gospels.

Daniel, Orville E. *A Harmony of the Four Gospels: The New International Version*. Grand Rapids, MI: Baker, 1996.

Other widely respected Gospel harmonies and parallels include:

Aland, Kurt. *Synopsis of the Four Gospels: Completely Revised on the Basis of the Greek Text of the Nestle-Aland 26th Edition and Greek New Testament 3rd Edition : The Text Is the Second Edition of the Revised Standard Version*. New York: American Bible Society, 1985.

Robertson, A. T., and John Albert Broadus. *A Harmony of the Gospels for Students of the Life of Christ: Based on the Broadus Harmony in the Revised Version*. New York: Harper & Bros., 1950.

Thomas, Robert L., and Stanley N. Gundry. *A Harmony of the Gospels, with Explanations and Essays: Using the Text of the New American Standard Bible*. San Francisco: Harper & Row, 1978.

Partial Scripture Index

Notes

Made in the USA
Middletown, DE
27 October 2022

13645579R00137